JOHN CHURTON COLLINS

THE LOUSE ON THE
LOCKS OF LITERATURE

JOHN CHURTON COLLINS

THE LOUSE
ON THE
LOCKS OF LITERATURE

ANTHONY KEARNEY

SCOTTISH ACADEMIC PRESS LIMITED
EDINBURGH
1986

First published 1986 by Scottish Academic Press

Copyright © Scottish Academic Press

ISBN   07073   0480 6

British Library Catologuing in Publication Data
Kearney, Anthony
John Churton Collins: the louse on the locks of literature.
1. Collins, John Churton   2. Critics—Great Britain—Biography
I. Title
820.9   PN75.C/

ISBN 0–7073–0480–6

Printed and bound in Great Britain by
Latimer Trend & Company Ltd, Plymouth

CONTENTS

	Acknowledgements	vii
	Introduction	ix
Chapter 1	Early Life: School and University	1
2	Getting on	18
3	University Extension Lecturing	36
4	The Symonds and Gosse Fracas	52
5	The Oxford Dispute	70
6	Three Books	88
7	The 'Saturday' Reviewer	105
8	The English Professor	120
9	The Last Campaign	137
10	Summing Up	150
	Appendix 1	168
	Appendix 2	171
	Appendix 3	174
	Select Bibliography	176
	Index	182

Frontispiece
John Churton Collins, 1848–1908
Permission of the Bodleian Library, Oxford.

ACKNOWLEDGEMENTS

I should like to thank all those who answered my queries about Collins over a long period of time, together with those who generously offered information without waiting to be asked. I should also like to thank the following institutions for allowing me to refer to materials in their collections: the University of Birmingham (notebooks and letters of John Churton Collins and university archives of the period 1900–1909); the Brotherton Library, University of Leeds (letters from Collins to Edmund Gosse); the Bodleian Library, University of Oxford (Collins' applications for chairs of English, Extension syllabuses and pamphlets); the Extra-Mural Department, University of London (reports, minutes and other papers relating to Collins' work for London Extension organizations). I am also indebted to the Trustees of the National Library of Scotland for my references to Collins' letters to Carlyle and William Blackwood, and to the Keeper of the Archives of the University of Oxford for my references to reports and minutes relating to Collins' dealings with the Oxford Extension Committee. I should also like to thank Yale University Press for allowing me to quote from Cecil Lang's edition of Swinburne's letters and Faber and Faber for allowing a quotation from T. S. Eliot's *Selected Essays*. Finally, I am grateful to the editors of the *British Journal of Educational Studies* and *Notes and Queries* for permission to reproduce material which first appeared in those journals. If there are any executors of materials used in this study from whom I have not obtained permission for brief quotations, I offer them my sincere apologies and assure them that every attempt was made to locate them.

In an attempt to give Collins the full scholarly treatment, I have been chiefly concerned with so-called primary sources, but I have also found some useful leads in the few secondary sources which touch on him. Apart from the books by Stephen Potter and John

Gross referred to in the Introduction, I should like to mention Phyllis Grosskurth's article on Collins in the *University of Toronto Quarterly* (April 1965) and D. J. Palmer's *The Rise of English Studies* (1965). Both these try to probe a little behind Collins' mad professor image and represent valuable—if insufficiently filled-out—attempts to understand different sides of Collins' career; namely the prickly reviewer and the educational campaigner. Ann Thwaite's *Edmund Gosse: A Literary Landscape* (1984) unfortunately appeared too late on the scene for me to make use of its full and excellent account of Gosse and his circle; an account which provides the definitive version of the Gosse-Collins fracas seen from the Gosse side of things. The aim of the present study is, of course, to give the Collins side of things on that and many other jarring encounters in the man's life.

INTRODUCTION

John Churton Collins is one of the most intriguing and paradoxical figures of the late Victorian literary world. Learned critic, energetic campaigner for English studies and inspiring lecturer, he also managed to quarrel with almost everyone of literary consequence he came into contact with, usually after reviewing their work. Collins, the 'new Macaulay' as he was called, was the most devastating reviewer of his day and his crushing remarks on books and authors led him into violent disputes with such people as Swinburne and Gosse and marginally less violent ones with a whole host of other writers and critics from Tennyson to Symonds and Saintsbury. Not surprisingly, Collins the reviewer was soon known as something other than the 'new Macaulay' in smart literary circles: Tennyson called him a 'louse on the locks of literature' while Theodore Watts-Dunton told him to his face that he was 'the most envious malignant man in Great Britain'. Collins in fact had a gift for attracting offensive nicknames: in the Gosse household, for example, he was known as 'shirt 'n collars' and elsewhere he was variously referred to as 'Random Tearem' (*The Oxford Magazine*), the 'demon-mole' (Richard Le Gallienne) and the 'Timon of critics' (Arthur Symons).

By and large this image of Collins as a savage reviewer (a sort of Jack the Ripper of the literary journals) and general troublemaker has hardened into a caricature over the years. Where he makes brief appearances in such books as Stephen Potter's *The Muse in Chains* (1937) or John Gross's *The Rise and Fall of the Man of Letters* (1969), for example, it is chiefly in the role of a demented and overbearing figure always on the warpath of imaginary rivals and enemies. But a quick glance at the only full-length biography of the man, the *Life and Memoirs of John Churton Collins* (1912) written by his son L. C. Collins, shows how much a travesty this is. Collins himself did much to encourage the caricature certainly but as the biography brings out there were many other sides to the man. If he offended some people by his brutal directness and cutting style, he remained a popular and impressive figure with several generations of students, colleagues and readers of his work. Collins was obviously a highly complex man; a compulsive fighter, an assertive critic and, above all, an insecure personality who felt the need to seek out and confront potentially hostile factions in the literary and educational fields. Yet despite this, as the biography shows, he gained the affection and respect of many people for his kindliness, sincerity, consistency and courage.

Giving Collins his due as a man is one purpose in writing a new study of him today but even more importantly his career spanning the fields of journalism, literary criticism, reviewing, Extension lecturing and university teaching puts us in touch with some vital areas of the cultural scene during the period 1875–1908. As a young Oxford graduate in the 1870s, Collins had precious few advantages or prospects when he arrived in London intent on a literary career but by sheer determination and skilful use of his abilities as a literary journalist and publicist he succeeded in transforming himself from impecunious nonentity to a figure of some substance in literary circles by the mid-1880s. This process of determined self-help brought him into contact (smooth or violent) with many famous Victorians. He met Carlyle and Browning and recorded their thoughts on various topics; he cultivated the friendship of Swinburne and Gosse; he corresponded with Matthew Arnold and other famous literary figures; through his campaigning for this or that cause he was in touch with a whole range of establishment figures (Gladstone, Morley and Goschen among them) and socially he met most of the literary world of the time. His survival and success as a man of letters at this time has its own special interest for literary historians and cultural critics.

But even more significant is his allied career as a teacher of (and propagandist for) English literature, first as a civil service coach, then as a University Extension lecturer and finally as Professor of English at Birmingham University between 1904 and 1908. Collins was a teacher of English literature at a crucial stage in its evolution as a respectable academic subject and, being Collins, he played a vital role in this evolution. During the 1880s he emerged as the leading spokesman in the campaign to establish the subject at

Oxford and almost singlehandedly turned the issue of the appointment of an English Professor there into a fierce national debate
about the nature and value of literary (as opposed to philological)
studies. The debate provoked a huge spate of letters to newspapers, articles, pamphlets and books on the subject in all of which
Collins was the dominant voice. His exploits on this front earned
him some flattering tributes to match the jibes and insults thrown
out by the literary world, though these are not often mentioned:
for example for the *University Extension Journal* he was the chief
inspirer of the 'new Humanist revival' in the educational world,
while for the American magazine *Harper's Weekly*, he was the
'relentless foe to the medieval spirit in English education'. Collins'
contribution to the English studies debate needs careful analysis
but there is no doubting his importance as a propagandist in the
movement which paved the way for the successful establishment
of English literature as a high level academic subject.

Collins in fact was never out of the news where English
literature and education were concerned from about 1885 until his
death in 1908. As an Extension lecturer he campaigned endlessly
for English literature and the Classics to be studied side by side; as
a reviewer for the *Saturday* in the 1890s he attacked dozens of books
aimed at the student market; later at Birmingham University, not
content with setting up a School of English to put the Oxford
English School in the shade, he campaigned for a School of
Journalism where young Collinses could be trained for their work
as public watchdogs and cultural critics. As a follower of Matthew
Arnold and as a precursor of F. R. Leavis and his associates,
Collins takes us in all kinds of interesting directions from the
metropolitan literary world to the stärker worlds of Extension
lecturing, newspaper offices and new provincial universities; all of
which he moved through with demonic energy and highminded
purpose.

L. C. Collins' biography of course is the basic sourcebook for all
this activity and it might be argued that there is no more to be said
on the matter. But the biography was written with the express
purpose of answering Collins' detractors and of showing him in
the best possible light. To do this L. C. Collins goes much too far in
the other direction, focusing on all his father's good points and
suppressing any awkward or inconvenient facts. He says nothing,

amazingly, about Collins' quarrel with Gosse (Gosse of course was still very much alive at the time the biography appeared), nothing about his unsuccessful application for the Merton Chair of English at Oxford in 1885 and nothing about his clash with London University in 1905–06. He also makes no attempt to assess his father's various achievements or to set them in their proper contexts. Understandably too he shies away from any too deep consideration of his father's personality beyond touching briefly on his sensitivity and acute depressions. Collins, in fact, had something of a knack for mixing his successes with extraordinary blunders and failures: for example his marriage in 1878 (about which L. C. Collins is desperately circumspect) seems to have been forced on him by the arrival of L. C. Collins into the world at a time when Collins senior had barely enough money to feed himself let alone support a wife and family. His death too was all of a piece with the rest of his sensational career being horribly sudden and looking very much like suicide.

The reason then for taking up Collins again is to try to see the man as he really was—avoiding both the distortions of the 'louse' image and the plaster saint of the L. C. Collins alternative—to make plain certain facts about his life and career and to assess his ideas and achievements as a teacher, literary propagandist and cultural critic in the context of his endless battles with philologists, aesthetes, dilettante scholars, literary cliques and academics. Only when this has been done can we get the proper measure of the man and his various successes and failures.

EARLY LIFE: SCHOOL AND UNIVERSITY

Unlike his well-known contemporaries, John Addington Symonds, Edmund Gosse and George Saintsbury, Collins left no substantial memoirs; all that remain are his occasional jottings and diary entries in notebooks and his habit of setting down his thoughts 'in any order, opening the volume at haphazard'[1] makes it difficult to piece together certain aspects of his life, especially in the early part. Luckily L. C. Collins' *Life and Memoirs of John Churton Collins* fills out much of the early background and this, together with the odd notebooks which survive, gives us a reasonably clear picture of the formative influences on Collins' life.[2]

John Churton Collins was born on 26 March 1848 (a suitably stormy year) at Bourton-on-the-Water, Gloucestershire, the eldest of three sons. His father, Henry Ramsay Collins, was a doctor who married a Maria Churton of Chester in 1847 and then set up practice in Gloucestershire. Henry Collins, in his grandson's account, was a kindly and gentle man, but he was also a hypochondriac and a dreamer. Bourton-on-the-Water turned out to be precisely the wrong place to start up a new medical practice, since it was already well supplied with doctors, and Henry Collins was soon led by worry and ill-health to take another disastrous step. Believing that a complete change of scene was necessary, he went off to Liverpool and signed on as ship's doctor on the *Carrier Dove*, which was about to leave for Melbourne, Australia. He intended to return to England as soon as possible, simply using the voyages as a means to regain his health. Unfortunately things worked out differently. Shortly after arriving in Melbourne he fell off a ladder and broke his thigh, and on recovering from this was almost immediately back in hospital with a chill. The chill rapidly developed into consumption and Henry Collins died in Melbourne on 6 June 1858 at the age of thirty-four, leaving his wife with three young children to provide for back in England.

Henry Collins' accident-prone brief life is of interest here because he evidently passed on some of his more alarming characteristics and tendencies to his eldest son. These include his hypochondria and his obvious inability to organize his affairs efficiently and satisfactorily. Throughout his life Collins suffered from recurring bouts of anxiety and depression, was hopelessly unworldly where money was concerned, and until his appointment to the Chair of English at Birmingham University in 1904, at the age of fifty-six, was without any secure means of employment but with a wife and seven children to support. There was always something Micawberish about Collins despite his more forceful qualities. The circumstances of his death also suggest—as in his father's case—that he was running away from problems he could no longer face.

Meanwhile back in 1858 the young Mrs Collins and her three children were fortunately rescued from disaster by her brother John Churton, an estate agent, J.P., and later High Sheriff of Flintshire. The Churtons, who were very comfortably off, provided for Mrs Collins and her children and sent the two older boys, John and Henry, first to the King's School Chester and then to a School in Ellesmere, where they remained until 1863.

John Churton Collins, who was his uncle's 'special favourite'[3] emerges from L. C. Collins' account of his early life as a strong-willed, lively and precocious character with a gluttonous appetite for reading and a talent for entertaining people with stories and recitations. By the time he was fifteen he had already read his way through wide tracts of English and classical literature and was writing poetry modelled on his favourite poets. His relatives clearly felt they had a young genius on their hands and Collins was given every encouragement to indulge his poetic gift. Dr Alexander Potts, later Headmaster of Fettes College Edinburgh, and a distant relative, wrote to him in highly flattering terms about his poetry saying

> When you ask me for a criticism on your poem, I am tempted to send you a eulogy instead, from my sympathy with your tastes and my surprise at the merit of your verses, when I think of your age—[4]

This letter also shows that Collins from an early age was already eager for recognition of his literary talents and keen to cultivate the best opinions. In fact the samples of his poems which L. C. Collins prints in his biography suggest that his *poetic* talent at any rate was nonexistent: he was a skilful imitator of poets he had read but certainly no genius. Nonetheless, as the following example shows, by the age of twelve he knew how to turn out a fair imitation of Dryden:

> As great Augustus, who, in ancient days,
> Crown'd his good actions with ten thousand lays;
> Who govern'd Rome, did all her greatness bring;
> And the good people loved their gracious King;—
> So have you ruled us with a gentle hand,
> And scatter'd blessings on this glorious land,
> So have you raised this country's name,
> That worlds lie prostrate at our awful fame. etc.
> (*A Panegyric: To Her Majesty Queen Victoria*)[5]

Effusions of this kind were sufficient to impress Collins' teachers and relatives and he in turn, encouraged by their response, began to think that he might give his life to poetry and literature. His uncle, the estate agent, however, was decidedly cool about this and clearly had other ideas for young Collins. From correspondence which passed between J. D. Day, the Headmaster of Ellesmere School, and Mrs Collins it is apparent that discussions took place about the possibility of Collins being directed towards the business world in some capacity or other—Uncle John was obviously applying pressure. Luckily for Collins, Day was sympathetic and towards the end of 1862 wrote to Mrs Collins in the following terms:

> I have had a long conversation and trial of your son's special qualities. I think he dislikes and is unfitted for the duties of a clerk in an office where *accounts* would be his work. His mind is, as you say, quite set on literary pursuits, and I find that he is decidedly clever in them and has already made by his own extra attention to them, very good and intelligent progress.
>
> He says he is very anxious to become a clergyman: I have said all in my power to combat this idea for the sake of testing him, but he comes back to the same conclusion.[6]

The suggestion that he wanted to become a clergyman may well have been a ruse on Collins' part in order to make sure that he was later allowed to go to university where he could follow up his literary interests (later events suggest this). If so, it worked very well. Day advised that Collins should leave Ellesmere and go on to some other school where he would get a better grounding in Classics and thus proceed to Oxford or Cambridge. Dr Potts, the schoolmaster relative, suggested the same course of action and recommended Rugby, where he himself was then teaching, as the right school for Collins. It was settled that Collins should enter Charles Evans' House at Rugby, when Evans was suddenly appointed headmaster of King Edward's School Birmingham; since Evans had been strongly recommended—he was an excellent classical scholar, a firm disciplinarian and a teacher whose pupils achieved good results[7]—Collins followed him to King Edward's School in the Autumn of 1863.

2

In view of Collins' later hectic involvement with educational issues, it can be pointed out that his own schooling during the 1860s took place at a time of radical questioning. A year after he entered King Edward's, the Clarendon Report on the nine famous public schools appeared and this was followed in 1868 by the Taunton Report which investigated the remainder of the secondary system in Britain, including of course King Edward's, Birmingham. Collins obviously took no interest in these enquiries at the time but he was later deeply involved with one of the questions at issue; this was the status of English in the secondary curriculum. English—and particularly English literature—was in a sad state of neglect in the 1860s: 'literature' in the public schools and in many of the endowed grammar schools meant Latin and Greek only, and even where, as in some schools, modern sides were being set up to prepare pupils for professional or commercial careers the Taunton Commission reported a marked lack of enthusiasm for English literature. At King Edward's, for example, where there was a 'modern' department, Latin still appeared more often than English on the timetable in the lower forms and English practically disappeared altogether higher up the school.[8] The same was true in other grammar schools to the professed regret of several witnesses to the Commission. This regret was shared by the Commissioners, who looked to English literature to infuse a new spirit in the Middle Classes—compounded of patriotism, moral uplift and heightened sensitivity—and they made their recommendation accordingly:

> Assuredly, it would be a most valuable result if anything like a real interest in English literature could be made general in England; and we cannot believe that English could not be studied in English schools with the same care and with the same effect as French is in French schools and German in Prussian schools.[9]

In the event English made its way into the secondary schools mainly as a useful examination subject, but the right Arnoldian line had been struck and within a few years Collins would be adding his own arguments to it, this time demanding that Oxford and Cambridge follow the schools' example.

As a potential university candidate, of course, Collins was placed in the 'classical' department at King Edward's and so received no formal teaching in English literature; a situation he makes no comment on and so was presumably happy with. Like most educated men of his day he took the classical priorities for granted, was contented early on to teach himself English literature and soon acquired an impressive knowledge of it (in fact it was a major stumbling block to the acceptance of English literature as a serious academic subject that so many educated men got it up for themselves). Collins at any rate was soon supplementing his classical reading with a good range of reading in English literature and during his first term at King Edward's took up Virgil, Horace, Lucretius, Spenser, Shakespeare, Milton, Pope, Akenside, Warton and Campbell. He modelled his own poetry on that of Pope and Campbell and was already laying the base for later researches into eighteenth-century literature. Reading English literature side by side with classical in this way also helped him to develop what became an obsessive concern with questions of literary influence and parallel and led him to insist that, wherever possible, ancient and modern literature must be studied together.

Collins' schoolboy notebooks show him as a determined, compe-

titive personality, with a strong sense of his own abilities and an
eagerness to take on authorities when he felt himself to be in the
right. One entry for example reads:

> Got up went to school, got down in verses but it was a cheat for he
> [the master] said 'sub' was not long and I know 2 verses from Virgil
> where it is long in one and short in another. Got full marks for my
> Greek. I said it very well indeed.[10]

Collins' passion for what he considered to be the truth was clearly
already well-developed by this time and he was easily outraged
when his knowledge of particular facts was challenged. At King
Edward's he was also already setting up as a critical expert,
someone who knew the difference between a fake and the real
thing—for example:

> Rumours are also circulating among the boys that Meredith has not
> written the 'Parrot' which I have mentioned before, but that he
> copied it out and put some lines of his own (sic), and that I have
> pointed out *right* every line that Meredith wrote and every line he
> altered or copied. I am glad the truth is coming out.[11]

Collins conceitedly always saw himself as a truth-teller. On
another occasion he prepared himself for the battles to come by
hammering the school magazine in the style of the *Quarterly Review*.

It would be unfair of course to draw too many conclusions from
these youthful jottings but they suggest well enough the prickly
and self-opinionated side to Collins' character which emerged
more strongly later on. L. C. Collins understandably does not
mention these notebook entries but he emphasizes Collins' passion
for literature which at times gave him an almost proprietorial
feeling about it. His delight in literature was also heightened by his
amazingly retentive memory which enabled him to remember
practically everything he had ever read. This talent was already in
evidence at King Edward's: on one occasion he managed to learn
thirty lines of *Paradise Lost* in a quarter of an hour,[12] and on
another astonished his cousin by reciting two thousand lines of
Virgil with barely a falter.[13] All this suggests a talent for showing-
off as well as precocity but Collins must have been less overbearing
than he sounds since people never tired of listening to his recitals.
He had an excellent voice—'with perfect enunciation and with a
curious haunting undertone of music' as someone later described

it[14]—and was always able to move and enthral an audience. In July 1866, at the King Edward's Speech Day, he 'brought down the house' with his recitation of Dryden's *Ode on St. Cecilia's Day*.[15] His later gifts as a teacher of literature obviously owed a good deal to such skilled performances.

3

Collins left King Edward's in 1868 and went up to Balliol College Oxford. L. C. Collins writes 'It is not clear why Balliol should have been selected',[16] but there was in fact a link between Balliol and King Edward's at this time. In 1865 the Balliol philospher, T. H. Green, was appointed an Assistant Commissioner to the Taunton Commission and was sent to write a special report on King Edward's.[17] Green impressed Evans, the Headmaster, and was later made a school governor, and so a link was formed between the school and Balliol which no doubt explains why Collins was sent there.

Collins himself unfortunately left no memoirs of his time at Balliol and L. C. Collins is not very informative either, but in fact, as is made plain by other sources, Balliol at this time was precisely the College for someone with Collins' literary interests. During a period of thirty years, A. H. Clough, J. C. Shairp, Matthew Arnold, F. T. Palgrave, Swinburne, Addington Symonds and Gerard Manley Hopkins had all been undergraduates there and Browning was elected an Honorary Fellow of the College in 1867. Both Browning and Swinburne were regular visitors to the College and Swinburne in particular had several 'enthusiastic worshippers' among the undergraduates.[18] Collins, who was always desperately eager to cultivate the acquaintance of literary genius, would certainly have been among these worshippers. His fellow students included Andrew Lang, W. H. Mallock, Herbert Asquith and Alfred Milner, and Collins, who no doubt felt the need to impress this company, soon began to affect the jaunty mannerisms of an up-and-coming poet and literary man: once installed in Balliol he dressed in a velveteen coat like a young aesthete and sauntered about Oxford with a deerhound called Prince doing little work on his formal studies but following up his literary interests and cultivating likeminded acquaintances. (Collins' aesthetic pose, however, was really nothing more than a pose—he later developed a violent hatred of the whole aesthetic movement.) Andrew Lang remembered him as a likeable and lively character: 'At that time', said Lang, 'Mr Collins always reminded me outwardly of Will Ladislas [sic] in the then new novel of "Middlemarch". He was slimly built and very active . . . and had a charming air of joy in life.'[19] Collins also impressed the Balliol students with his skills as a literary raconteur and reciter. Asquith later told a University Extension gathering of his gifts in this direction:

> I do not believe that the subject of English literature could be handled by any more competent man than Mr Churton Collins in the whole of Great Britain. I well remember how, twenty years ago, when Mr Collins and I were at Balliol together, I have often sat into the small hours of the morning while my friend poured forth out of the flood-gates of a most capacious memory treasures both new and old.[20]

This image of Collins is a long way removed from the later repulsive image prompted by his hatchet reviews; with many people he managed to retain a cheerful, easy-going relationship and he obviously struck his Oxford contemporaries as a friendly, out-going figure, giving no hint of the envy and vindictiveness he was later charged with. His only apparent handicaps at this stage were his shortsightedness and his frequent absentmindedness which gave him an agreeably eccentric air.

Collins' cavalier attitude to his Oxford studies, together with his casual indifference to money, soon however brought him into conflict with his uncle. His uncle, who of course was still supporting him financially, complained bitterly about Collins' easy-going assumptions and the final straw was Collins' announcement that he had changed his mind about becoming a clergyman—the sole justification, in the uncle's eyes, for Collins being at Oxford at all. A blazing row finally broke out and from 1872 onwards, after Collins' graduation, there was no further contact between them. This quarrel was the first of several similar ones when Collins found himself falling out with someone he had previously liked and respected, suggesting that he felt a compulsion to reject certain friends and allies after a while (Gosse and Swinburne are later instances), coming to see them either as obstacles to his own development or as representatives of things he disapproved of. Where his uncle was concerned, however, the rift caused Collins some pain and remained a source of guilt and unease until Uncle John's death in 1884.[21] Despite his regrets, though, he plainly felt the need to rid himself of any dependence on this domineering father-figure and man of business.

4

Collins' academic career at Oxford shows that his uncle had cause for anxiety. In 1870, in Classical Moderations, he scraped only a poor third and in his final examinations in the School of Law and History two years later managed only a second class.[22] At Oxford at this time there were five final Examination Schools: Theology, Law and History, Mathematics, Natural Science and Literae Humaniores (Greats). In Collins' time it was quite common for undergraduates to take more than one Final School—normally Greats first and then some other School. Collins, however, with all his love of classical literature, decided not to take Greats but chose the easier alternative of Law and History. The School of Law and History was in effect a school of modern studies, involving aspects of political, economic and legal thought and making less demands than Greats, where the main emphasis was on Logic, Moral and Political Philosophy and Ancient History. By opting for the School of Law and History, Collins gave himself more time to read English and classical literature or whatever took his fancy. He might also have been suggesting to his uncle that if he did not enter the Church he might take up Law. He perhaps thought seriously about this for a time and when he moved to London in 1872 took rooms in the Middle Temple and may even have attended some lectures there.[23]

Collins' notebooks during his Oxford years contain some jottings on his formal studies—Roman Law, English and European history and so on—but they are fuller of literary jottings, with notes of books read and copied-out extracts from histories of English and European literature including Thomas Warton's *History of English Poetry* (1774–78) and Henry Hallam's *Introduction to the Literature of Europe* (1837–39). Collins' reading was fairly unsystematic but he ranged very widely in his researches and dabblings. A typical notebook entry on 16 December 1871, for example, records him reading Thomas More, Flecknoe's *Epigrams*, Henry More, and some observations on Queen Elizabeth and her court by Sir Robert Naunton in a volume called *Fragmenta Regalia*. This list shows Collins' already well-developed taste for anything remotely literary or historical and might suggest he was a mere bookworm. In fact though, while he certainly liked to follow up the footnotes of literary history and was driven by curiosity to turn up odds and ends in well-stocked libraries, his overriding interest in literature as a reflection of life made him a critic and biographer rather than a scholarly pedant. Not surprisingly in his final examinations he 'amazed the examiners with the extent of his reading and prodigious memory' but sadly disappointed them with his knowledge of the set topics; consequently he missed the high honours he seemed capable of.[24] Had there been a School of English at Oxford at this time, that would have been a different matter. In 1873, the year after he graduated, Oxford edged a fraction towards this by making English one of the subjects for the pass degree.[25] For Collins, however, there was no chance to make direct use of all that compulsive reading in the highways and byways of English literature.

Despite the unsuitable courses (or despite his unsuitability for what was offered), Collins was at Oxford at a time of important changes in the University. Since the 1850s indeed widespread reforms had been taking place, involving the abolition of religious tests, the throwing open of fellowships and scholarships to competition and the widening of academic studies for the first degree; all of which gradually transformed the University from a semi-monastic establishment of learning (cum-polite finishing school) to a training ground for the professions and the public service. Moreover, through the new secondary schools examinations supervised by the University, and through the University Extension Movement, Oxford, like Cambridge, was progressively brought more fully into the mainstream of public life. Collins' own later career as a campaigner and reformer—and particularly his demands for an English School at Oxford—can be best understood in the context of these general developments: Oxford by the time

Collins' campaigns were underway was already taking responsibility for certain national educational concerns; Collins was anxious to press the University into giving the study of English literature further status and prestige by setting up its own English school.

Collins of course only developed his arguments for English studies long after he left Oxford but he certainly received some encouragement as a campaigner from his contacts with the famous Benjamin Jowett. Jowett, who became Master of Balliol in 1870, was not only keen to make Balliol the best college in Oxford but was also strongly committed to wider educational reforms. During the 1850s he had been a member of the committee which drew up the curriculum for the new Indian Civil Service examinations (giving special importance to English literature) and during the 1860s he was concerned with questions connected with university reforms, secondary education and the Extension Movement.[26] As a liberal Churchman he was also a leading figure (at Oxford a notorious one) in that mid-century effort to reinterpret Christian dogma and if necessary discard it where modern criticism showed it to be dubious or nonsensical. As a teacher (he became Regius Professor of Greek at Oxford in 1854), Jowett was a firm believer in the value of a humane education and, like other literary humanists admired by Collins, was more concerned with literature and philosophy than with minute questions of philology. M. L. Clarke writes of him: 'for him the function of the scholar was to bring Greek ideas into contact with the modern world, and the purpose of university education was to produce not scholars or researchers but statesmen and men of the world.'.[27] Collins' later career as teacher and literary campaigner was clearly modelled on this idea.

Collins own relationship with Jowett, however, seems to have been an uneasy one. There is no mention in Collins' memoirs—as there is in Mallock's[28]—of invitations to breakfast or dinner to meet distinguished guests like Browning and Swinburne, and no mention of any special interest shown by Jowett in Collins' later career. On hearing of Jowett's death in 1893, Collins wrote in his notebook:

> Another landmark gone—this, October 6th 1893, is Jowett's first night in the grave—a familiar figure in my past life: kind and good

he must have been to others: and a man to respect and admire—my
experience much otherwise.[29]

This suggests, if not an outright quarrel, at least a certain coolness
in the relationship. Collins no doubt was a disappointment to
Jowett, who always looked for tangible successes in Balliol men,
and while he gave him a degree of support in his campaign for
English literature he clearly disapproved of Collins' polemics.[30]
Probably Jowett found Collins too arrogant and quirky to get on
with once he had left Oxford, though he admired his literary
scholarship and wrote references for him when he applied for
university posts. Whatever their personal relationship, however,
Collins, with his faith in literary education and mission to reform,
was an unmistakable product of Jowett's Balliol.

5

Meanwhile, at Oxford, Collins' religious attitudes, till then safely
orthodox, were beginning to undergo some changes. This was
hardly surprising since Balliol under Jowett in the early 1870s was
a hive of questions and doubts where religion was concerned.
Mallock in his memoirs tells the story of the sensational suicide of a
student during his (Mallock's) first term at Balliol: 'He was a poor
Scotch student of a deeply religious character, who had found, so
his friends reported, that the faith of his childhood had been taken
from him by Jowett's sceptical teachings, and who had ended by
cutting his throat with a razor in Port Meadow.'[31] Balliol, in
Mallock's account of it, was certainly no place for anxious
believers; not only Jowett but 'Nearly all the Balliol dons—even
those who never spoke of religion—seemed to start with the same
foregone conclusion, that the dogmatic theology of the Churches
was as dead as the geocentric astronomy.'[32] Those not driven to
despair in all this upset and doubt turned for reassurance elsewhere. Some, like Collins, found uplift and guidance in Carlyle,
others in T. H. Green whose Hegelian brand of theism, if
intractable in detail, seemed to offer a philosophically respectable
basis for religious belief detached from Church teaching. For
Green God was an immanent power or spirit inherent in every-

thing and progressively realizing itself in human life and thought[33]—a notion which of course allowed anxious doubters to reject dogmas they could no longer accept while maintaining their faith in an ultimate spiritual reality. Equally importantly, Green also taught the value of a life of earnest self-improvement, self-sacrifice and social duty which, even more forcefully than his Hegelian philosophy, caught the imagination of Collins' generation. Thanks to Green, they were able to 'revive that spiritual fervour which they had inherited from earlier generations but against which the doubts of the new age had anaesthetized them'[34] and to find fulfilment in a life of good works and moral endeavour.

Collins apparently found Carlyle's writings more to his taste than Green's but he certainly came under Green's influence while he was at Balliol. After Green's death in 1882, he wrote: 'for two or three terms he was my College Tutor. No man had greater influence or was more deeply respected by the best men of my time'.[35] Green naturally enough could not answer all the doubts worrying people at the time (and the question of a 'future state' after death continued to worry Collins for the rest of his life) but his philosophical idealism and his belief in a progressive development towards ultimate enlightenment made its impact on Collins, as can be seen in a letter he wrote years later to his friend Mrs Edmund Luce:

> For myself I must own that the longer I live, and the more my experience grows, the more dense and impenetrable becomes the mystery of life. I mean the relation of God to the individual and the question of a future state . . . With regard to Christianity I believe it contains more essential truth, moral and spiritual, than any other religion which has taken form among men, but if you were to ask me whether it be final I should hesitate to say so. All truth, on this earth at least, is progressive, requiring progressive development to realize it.[36]

Like many other thoughtful Victorians of literary bent, Collins turned increasingly to literature for sustenance and uplift. Taking his cue from Carlyle here rather than Green (most likely from his remarks on writers and literature in *On Heroes, Hero-Worship and the Heroic in History* (1841)) Collins came to see literature in quasi-religious terms as 'the revelation of the eternal, the unchanging and the typical which underlies the unsubstantial and ever-dissolving empire of matter and time'.[37] The great writers were similarly elevated to the status of supreme teachers, speaking to the 'spiritual and moral nature of man' and contributing in unique ways to 'the solution of man's three great problems—what is he to do, what can he know, for what may he hope?'[38] By great writers, of course, Collins, like Carlyle, included all the great philosophers, prophets and poets in world history as well as the select English band of Shakespeare, Milton, Wordsworth, and so on.

It can be seen from this that Collins also owed a debt to Matthew Arnold for his lofty, religiose view of literature. Literature, and especially Poetry (always spelt with a Capital 'P' in this context), became for Collins the greater interpreter, sustainer and consoler in life and when describing its value in lectures and essays he powerfully outdid Arnold in making it the new panacea—for example—

> Now Poetry, not the sense-pampering siren which too often usurps her name, but Poetry in her excellence and majesty is the incarnation of ideal truth, the breath and finer spirit, as Wordsworth puts it, of all knowledge . . . She will corroborate, she will fortify, she will extend all that is vital and precious, not merely in the teaching of the Creed of creeds, but in the teaching of every creed which has taken form among the children of men. Other missions she has, many other missions, but this is the highest.[39]

Despite the grand Romantic rhetoric here (an amalgam of Wordsworth, Shelley, Carlyle and Arnold), there was nothing merely histrionic about Collins' feeling for literature: literature in effect became his surrogate religion, which explains how, in later life, he came to see the teaching of literature as his real mission in life.

In the summer of 1872, however, Collins as yet had no obvious mission in life and no clear prospects either. He took his degree on 20 June and for some days afterwards wandered around Oxford in a kind of daze not knowing what to do next. Obviously he would have liked to have stayed on in Oxford permanently, perhaps doing some private coaching to support himself (a College fellowship being out of the question), but mainly just spending his time in the libraries, idling his way through ancient and modern literature, making notes towards scholarly publications, and writing poetry. However there were more pressing needs; his uncle was no longer supporting him financially and besides his developing social conscience told him he ought to make some use of his abilities in the world beyond Oxford. After a few days of indecision, Collins finally took the obvious step and decided to look for literary, educational and journalistic opportunities in London—precisely the step most literary-minded, hard-up young graduates took. Collins, however, in a typical piece of high drama later claimed that he had received some special calling in this matter. L. C. Collins tells the story as follows:

> when the time came for leaving the University, he found himself in a very hopeless position, having no idea where to go or what to do, but just managing to scrape along by 'coaching'. As he was wandering about Oxford one day, he had a sudden desire to go into St. Giles' Church. Though not a religious man in the full sense of the word, he always had a most reverent, almost superstitious regard for churches—not a church-goer, he loved to go in when the church was empty, and to roam about. On this occasion he wandered in for some deeper reason—he wanted inspiration. He went up to the Bible lying on the lectern, opened it, and at once put his finger, without looking, at a place on the newly-opened page. It happened to be Acts ix. 6—'Arise and go into the city, and it shall be told thee what thou must do.'[40]

This sounds at first like a wild attempt on Collins' part to justify his decision to drift into London literary life without any positive direction in mind. But more likely Collins had some deeper need to see himself as marked out for some special mission in life. Not surprisingly in the Oxford of this time, with the teachings of Jowett and Green in the air, many young graduates felt a strong desire to be called to some serious work or purpose.[41] In Collins' case, the call may have been vague enough but certainly his later career as a teacher, campaigner and reformer suggests that he felt himself to be fulfilling some high moral purpose. After rejecting the idea of ordination, he felt the need for some equally serious calling.

At the age of twenty-four then Collins could look back on his life with mixed feelings. On the negative side he had squandered his opportunities where prizes and honours were concerned—

something he would have cause to regret later when he began applying for university posts—and he had also quarrelled with his uncle. But on the positive side he had cultivated his literary interests, had impressed many of his contemporaries, and had been able to meet distinguished men of letters. Jowett may not have included him in his breakfast and dinner parties but Collins was forward enough to make his own contacts—for example in July 1872 he proudly recorded the fact that he had had lunch with Robert Browning: 'He is a splendid man.'[42] He had also developed strong ties with Oxford itself, and though he left the University in 1872 in a sense he never left it emotionally; throughout his life he spent part of every vacation in Oxford, using the libraries and renewing old friendships, and twice applied (unsuccessfully) for chairs of English there. Like Arnold he admired Oxford in its idealized and sentimentalized form, while being critical of its academic practices. In his later polemical writings, Oxford was alternately the ideal university and a disgrace in the context of national education, depending on his particular mood and intention. Had Collins been appointed to an Oxford chair no doubt his attitude would have been unreservedly approving; as it was, through what he saw as rejection and betrayal, he developed a more ambivalent viewpoint, sometimes attacking Oxford for its reactionary attitudes, sometimes admiring it, like Arnold, for being 'still true to the ideal, still true to the beautiful'.[43] Whatever his later course of life beyond the University, he found it difficult to get Oxford out of his system.

NOTES

1   L. C. Collins, *Life and Memoirs of John Churton Collins*, 1912, p. 38.
2   There are four surviving notebooks kept in the library of Birmingham University.
3   L. C. Collins, op. cit., p. 8.
4   Ibid., p. 9.
5   Ibid., pp. 297–98.
6   Ibid., p. 11.
7   T. W. Hutton, *King Edward's School Birmingham 1552–1952*, Oxford, 1952, pp. 87–88.
8   *Taunton Commission Report*, 1868, III, 280–83.
9   Ibid., I, 25.
10 Notebooks, 28 October 1863.

11   Ibid., 29 October 1863.

12   Ibid., 8 November 1863.

13   L. C. Collins, op. cit., p. 13.

14   Ibid., p. 287.

15   Ibid., p. 15.

16   Ibid., p. 16.

17   T. W. Hutton, op. cit., pp. 48–49.

18   W. H. Mallock, *Memoirs of Life and Literature*, 1920, pp. 55 ff. Mallock
     provides a lively account of Balliol life during Collins' time there.

19   L. C. Collins, op. cit., p. 17.

20   Ibid., p. 62.

21   Ibid., p. 78.

22   *The Balliol College Register*, ed. Sir Ivo Elliott, 1934, p. 52.

23   L. C. Collins, op. cit., p. 44.

24   Ibid., p. 18.

25   C. H. Firth, *The School of English Language and Literature*, Oxford, 1909,
     p. 21.

26   Geoffrey Faber, *Jowett: A Portrait with a Background*, 1957, p. 353.

27   M. L. Clarke, *Classical Education in Britain 1500–1900*, Cambridge,
     1959, p. 103.

28   W. H. Mallock, op. cit., pp. 53–54.

29   L. C. Collins, op. cit., p. 131.

30   Jowett, for example, disapproved of Collins' treatment of Gosse. See
     his letter to Collins dated 6 February 1888. Balliol College library.

31   W. H. Mallock, op. cit., p. 60.

32   Ibid., p. 61.

33   See Peter Gordon and John White, *Philosophers as Educational
     Reformers*, 1979, p. 20.

34   Ibid., p. 23.

35   L. C. Collins, op. cit., p. 53.

36   Ibid., p. x.

37   J. C. Collins, *Studies in Poetry and Criticism*, 1905, p. 265.

38   L. C. Collins, op. cit., p. 316.

39   J. C. Collins, *Studies in Shakespeare*, 1904, pp. 133–34.

40   L. C. Collins, op. cit., pp. 20–21.

41   According to Frederic Harrison many Oxford graduates at this time
     fancied they had a call, 'though from what or whom, to what or
     whither' they had little idea. *Autobiographic Memoirs*, 2 vols., 1911, I,
     110.

42   Notebooks, 11 July 1872.

43   *The Posthumous Essays of John Churton Collins*, ed. L. C. Collins, 1912, p.
     173.

CHAPTER TWO

GETTING ON

Like many other hard-up graduates with a taste for literature, Collins arrived in London in 1872 hoping to break into literary journalism but, for the time being, despite the lunch with Browning, he lacked the contacts to make any headway. Unlike Edmund Gosse, who through the right connexions managed to find easy niches in the British Museum and the Board of Trade, and unlike Andrew Lang, who after a spell as an Oxford don moved effortlessly into the world of smart reviewing,[1] Collins took much longer to establish himself. For a time he spent part of every week doing private coaching in Oxford while looking out for openings in London but nothing showed up. At one point in fact things looked so bad that he was reduced to addressing envelopes at 2/6 per thousand and seemed likely to join the ranks of the literary down-and-outs. No doubt his uncle took grim satisfaction in this state of affairs.

Things took a turn for the better, however, when newspapers started to accept his miscellaneous pieces of writing (he received his first fee from the *Globe* on 3 August 1872),[2] and for the next few years he wrote many odds and ends for the *Globe* and the *Daily News*, writing about such things as curious London characters and slum life. In search of material, he visited such places as Johnson's opium den (made famous by Dickens in the opening chapter of *Edwin Drood*) and talked with thieves and other social outcasts, sometimes taking up what he saw as cases of injustice.[3] Thus early on he developed a strong interest in criminal life which led him throughout his career to follow up a succession of famous trials and unsolved cases—in the course of things he interviewed the Tichborne claimant and William Roupell the forger, took a keen interest in the Ripper murders, and was a frequent visitor to police stations and morgues.[4] In part this suggests a morbid obsession with crime (though by no means a rare one in Victorian London) but much more a fascination with the character and life of anyone famous: Collins had an overpowering curiosity in this direction and was immensely knowledgeable on the subject of famous people—criminal or otherwise—filing away facts about where they lived and died in addition to what they did and were like. As L. C. Collins reports, he was a great frequenter of cemeteries, knowing the 'last resting places of all the most notable people in history' and comprising in himself 'a veritable Who's Who in the cemeteries'.[5] A mania for facts and details about the lives of extraordinary men, all effortlessly committed to memory, became one of Collins' chief assets or foibles as journalist and historian from his early days in London.

Writing newspaper articles may have been a pleasant pastime for Collins but it scarcely provided enough money to live on. Consequently he was soon looking out for supplementary sources of income from private coaching. Casual work of this sort eventually brought him to the notice of William Baptiste Scoones who ran a coaching establishment in Garrick Street, and in 1874 Collins began to work for Scoones as a tutor in English literature and Classics preparing candidates for Civil Service examinations. Collins was always grateful to Scoones for taking him on to his staff and hearing of Scoones' death in 1906 he wrote:

> He gave me my first lift in life, and shrewdly believed in me, trusting me with work done only by very distinguished University men, and giving me much of the English Literature and Classics for the Indian Civil Service and Home Civil Service candidates. I always found him honest and straightforward, and very kindly . . . I shall always think of him gratefully.[6]

Collins' affection for Scoones—perhaps as a kind of substitute uncle—is shown by the fact that he continued to work for him for fourteen years, long after his real need for such work had passed. It was here that Collins got his first opportunity to develop his talent for teaching and to think about educational issues. It was said of the Civil Service Examinations that they required only the regurgitation of literary facts, but Collins always spoke up for the Indian Civil Service syllabus at least. The main principles of this syllabus had been laid down in 1855 by a committee of which Macaulay and Jowett were members and the best thing about it, so far as Collins was concerned, was the importance it gave to English literature. In his polemical articles he often referred to this fact when berating the universities for neglecting the subject.[7] Collins' students at Scoones were often graduates of Oxford and Cambridge who, like himself, had never studied English literature formally and most of them, as the repeated testimonies in L. C. Collins' book show, remained grateful to him for his lively teaching and stimulus. Whatever the limitations of examination coaching, Collins was unfailingly interesting on the subject of literature and could always count on former students to write grateful references for him. Stephen Phillips, whose reputation as a poet was extraordinarily high in the 1890s, later told Collins that he first got his love of verse from his 'classes at Scoones'.[8]

2

Collins' haphazard way of jotting down often undated notes about his activities makes it difficult to be sure just when things happened or in what order, but in addition to his journalism and his coaching during the early 1870s he was also starting to make some literary contacts. He had already met Browning while he was still at Oxford and some time in 1874 was writing to Carlyle asking if he could meet him. Carlyle evidently granted this interview—and probably another soon afterwards—since L. C. Collins prints an undated report of it. Collins' two letters to Carlyle[9] are repulsively effusive and flattering, though the flattering letter to a great man was of course the established way of getting on in literary London.[10] Collins addresses Carlyle as 'Dear Master', speaks of himself as 'a young graduate of Balliol', and begs the favour of meeting someone 'who has been to him his only Guide through a bewildered life.' The grovelling tone of this might suggest that Collins was simply ingratiating himself in order to make use of his contact with Carlyle later, but it is more likely that, in this case at least, his grovelling flattery was simply the expression of his genuine admiration for Carlyle's genius. Like many other earnest but anxious young men of his generation, Collins turned for inspiration and uplift to Carlyle's writings and found in them more reassurance than could be found in contemporary Church teaching.

Carlyle agreed to meet Collins and they talked at length of life and literature; or rather Carlyle talked and the young Balliol graduate took notes. With typical absentmindedness Collins wrote down Carlyle's words in pencil and they almost faded away before he got round to copying them up in ink. Carlyle evidently was in excellent form: he castigated Darwin and the novelist Ouida, described Swinburne and his school as a 'curious growth', and said he thought little of George Eliot, Dickens and Scott. He also referred to the modern age as 'a miserable chaotic confused mass of lies and rubbish which will swallow up everything unless it please God to raise up some great sperrit'. (A comment which probably stirred Collins with his sense of calling and mission.) Most of all, of course, Carlyle praised Goethe and the Germans for their literary and philosophical insights and he concluded the interview by giving Collins some sound advice:

> He told me to read *German*—read German at once, they are above everything necessary. You must admit *them*, the Germans, into the gallery of your Gods—(I telling him how I clung to the Greek). I asked him whether the presence of ambition implied the power to carry it out—he took refuge in Goethe and said, you know what Goethe says, 'our wishes are often presentiments of our capabilities.' His advice was—stick to some defined purpose—good or bad: 'a man without a purpose is soon down at zero'—better to have a bad purpose than no purpose at all.[11]

Collins later came to think less highly of Carlyle (see Appendix 3), but at this time when his beliefs were still forming and his purpose in life was not yet clear Carlyle's moral assertiveness was a source of comfort to the anxious young Balliol graduate. He was obviously completely sincere when he told Carlyle he had been guided by him through worries and doubts. As for Carlyle's advice, Collins still clung to the Greeks, only coming to learn German later in life, but the comment on ambition must have given him great satisfaction. His uncle and his Oxford tutors may have been disappointed with him up to this point but Collins intended to show them that he had plenty of ambition and drive in store.

Collins' first ventures as a serious man of letters, however, had ludicrously mixed results. His first actual publication—a 'pot-boiler' L. C. Collins calls it[12]—was a book called *Sir Joshua Reynolds as a Portrait Painter*, published by Macmillan in 1874. Reynolds was another genius admired by Collins, though according to his son he knew nothing at all about the technicalities of art. How he persuaded the publishers to accept his services is not clear, but in any case he merely supplied brief commentaries for a collection of twenty of Reynolds' portraits. His next attempt to get something into print was a fiasco. On 30 October 1874, he sent off an article to *Blackwood's Magazine* (a friend of Collins, a Mr Ormond, knew the editor well): the article was in essence a collection of anecdotes about famous Oxford men, including De Quincey, industriously gathered by Collins in Oxford libraries and elsewhere. Soon afterwards the editor expressed cautious interest in the article and Collins replied in a second letter saying he would be delighted to submit more work to *Blackwood's*, adding 'Need I say how much I reverence the very name of your magazine & how proud I should be to work for it.'[13]

This was the smooth prelude to what turned out to be a protracted and frustrating experience for Collins. The editor prevaricated, was not sure what form the article should take, found the ending 'puzzlingly incoherent'; and eventually Collins recast the article, sent it back, received the proofs and corrected them, but heard nothing more from *Blackwood's*. By October 1877 Collins was justifiably getting annoyed: *Blackwood's* had had his article for three years had set it up in type and the proofs had been corrected; it was not unreasonable to ask when it was going to appear. In November *Blackwood's* finally deigned to reply, enclosing a cheque, but saying that the article was still not fully acceptable in its recast form. Nothing further was heard about the article and it never appeared. Amazingly in the circumstances, Collins sent another piece to *Blackwood's* on 17 June 1878 entitled 'A New Study of Tennyson' and referred to his earlier piece: 'You may remember me as the hapless author of a thing called Athenaeus Oxoniensis about which we had some trouble.' The polite tone, however, did nothing to speed up negotiations over this new article and within a few months, after several enquiries about it, Collins wrote angrily to *Blackwood's* telling them that he

had never 'met with such gross discourtesy': 'I am not an idle
amateur. I am a hard working literary man, and as I told your
editor, the loss of a manuscript is the loss of money.' Collins
eventually sent the Tennyson article to the *Cornhill* but still
submitted pieces to *Blackwood's* with stubborn hopefulness. His
final try came in July 1905 when he offered them an article on a
little-known early nineteenth-century man of letters, John Carne,
sardonically reminding them that he had been paid over thirty
years earlier for an article that was 'still under consideration'!

This whole farcical episode certainly suggests Collins' idiotic
persistency; it surely ought to have been clear to him that
Blackwood's did not want his literary anecdotes and other articles,
though their behaviour in the matter was obviously inexcusable.
But it also highlights the extent to which he had to fight his way
painfully towards literary success during his early years in London
and helps to explain his instinctive hostility to men of letters like
Symonds and Gosse who moved much more smoothly and easily
into recognition. And, since success without connexions was hard
to come by, Collins would not refrain from reaching for a little
notoriety from time to time by exposing the fraudulent practices
of the literary world.

3

Despite his later contempt for the literary cliques and 'log-rollers',
Collins quickly set about making his own influential contacts in the
early 1870s. His meeting with Carlyle came about through his
reverence for Carlyle's genius rather than from any thought that
there might be other gains in it, but his approach to Swinburne in
1873 or 1874—as so often with Collins the date is not clear—
certainly involved some ulterior motives. True Collins remained a
devout admirer of Swinburne's poetry throughout his life—
particularly of *Atalanta in Calydon*—but contact with Swinburne
also offered him all kinds of openings and opportunities as others,
including Gosse, had already found. The approach was made
when Collins, half-calculatingly at least, decided he would like to
edit the Plays and Poems of Cyril Tourneur, the Jacobean
dramatist. He wrote to Swinburne telling him of this project and

certainly aware of the fact that Swinburne was strongly interested in Tourneur and had in fact considered editing him. Swinburne was delighted to hear of this proposal, congratulated him on being the man chosen to revive an interest in Tourneur, and offered to lend him a 1608 copy of the *Revenger's Tragedy* in his possession.[14]

From this point on Swinburne took the keenest interest in the gradual progress of the edition and enjoyed discussing knotty textual problems with Collins, mediating between him and another Tourneur expert, A. B. Grosart ('more of an enthusiast and bookworm than a critic', Swinburne called him).[15] When the edition finally appeared in 1878, it was naturally dedicated to Swinburne.

The *Plays and Poems of Cyril Tourneur* was Collins' first major literary project and he clearly took some pains with it. Unfortunately he was a complete novice in textual matters and later editors came to find it a careless and inadequate edition—this was the fate of more than one of Collins' editorial efforts. A recent editor of Tourneur's *The Atheist's Tragedy* highlights his shortcomings in this respect as follows:

> This is a very careless edition with words omitted, and with many unexplainable departures from the quarto. Collins made no attempt to collate different copies of the quarto, and this was particularly unfortunate because he appears to have used one of the uncorrected copies . . .[16]

As an ambitious man of letters Collins may have felt that textual matters were mere pedantries beneath him, or perhaps his short-sightedness and absentmindedness got the better of his editorial brain. In either case he would have done better to have left serious editing alone. On the other hand, his critical introduction to Tourneur was clear, sharp and well-informed and gained high praise both at the time and later. According to T. S. Eliot writing in 1930, 'Churton Collins's introduction to the works is by far the most penetrating interpretation of Tourneur that has been written.'[17]

For Collins himself of course the most satisfying result of the Tourneur project was that it brought friendship with Swinburne. Within a short time Swinburne wanted to drop the Mr from the correspondence—'I don't see why you should *Mr* me unless you

esteem my friendship less than I do yours.'[18]—and as time passed
the tone of his letters became increasingly informal and jocular. By
1880 Collins was paying frequent visits to Swinburne's house in
Putney where he listened to Swinburne reading his poems, met
distinguished literary figures, and sometimes took walks with
Swinburne over Putney Heath talking literature to his heart's
content. An entry in Collins' notebook for 28 April 1880 shows
how he had moved up in the literary world by this time:

> I must jot down this. This evening I went by invitation to hear
> Swinburne read his new volume of poems. There were present,
> Theodore Watts, Austin Dobson, Arthur O'Shaughnessy, William
> Rossetti, and Philip Marston. He read almost all the volume with
> the exception of the long Ode to Victor Hugo. Returned by 11.30
> train with O'Shaughnessy, Rossetti and Marston. We talked of
> Walt Whitman in the train. I walked with Rossetti from Waterloo
> almost to the University College, Gower Street. We talked princi-
> pally about the Italian poets. Said he and his father preferred Tasso
> to Ariosto—we had a very animated conversation.[19]

Swinburne clearly delighted in Collins' enthusiasm for literature
and Collins was plainly flattered to be moving in such elite literary
circles. This friendly relationship persisted through the early
1880s, despite the odd argument about literary matters—for
example, on one occasion Swinburne attacked Carlyle and Collins
strongly defended him.[20] Generally the atmosphere was extremely
cordial with Collins admiring Swinburne's poems and Swinburne
repaying the debt with praise of Collins' articles. For example
when Collins wrote two educational articles in 1886 Swinburne
wrote to him saying 'I never read anything with more absolute
sympathy or with more sincere gratitude ... The reasoning is
unanswerable, and the expression unsurpassable.'[21] However, as
we shall see, by this time Collins was ready to shake off the
Swinburne contact.

Another vital contact for Collins at this time was Edmund
Gosse, whom he most likely met through Swinburne.[22] Gosse was
already well-established in the literary world by the late 1870s,
having succeeded as a writer and critic by a mixture of talent, hard
work and the careful cultivation of the right connexions. After a
stern upbringing with his puritanical father—recounted in his one
really fine book *Father and Son*—Gosse came to London at the age

of seventeen determined to make his name as a man of letters. Through Charles Kingsley's help he was appointed to a position in the cataloguing section of the British Museum and found the time there to educate himself in English and other literatures. He also published collections of poems at his own expense, sending them off to famous writers for approval, and energetically pursued editors, critics and publishers. By his determination and flair, by his critical articles, poems, translations and reviews, not to mention his growing number of influential friends, Gosse was just the type of literary man to impress an up-and-coming young hopeful like Churton Collins. At this stage too in the late 1870s Gosse had not yet tried his hand at subjects which would prove to be beyond him.

Like Swinburne, Gosse was obviously taken with Collins' zest for literature and was flattered by his attentions, and, like Swinburne again, he encouraged him in his literary projects and introduced him to the right people. Collins' few surviving letters to Gosse show him properly grateful to Gosse for his friendship and help: he appreciated Gosse's attempts to bring his articles into notice, told him he delighted in his company, admired his poems, and suggested various outings including a visit to some opium dens he had recently discovered.[23] Later on, when Collins savaged Gosse in the *Quarterly Review*, he was accused of brutally mistreating an old friend, yet it is unlikely that the two men were ever really very close. The letters in fact show tensions and upsets from the start. Both men were hypersensitive to imagined slights and insults and Collins was soon apologizing to Gosse for having seemed to cut him dead in the British Museum: 'I am very blind & very absent', he explained, '& have even been hit by a stick & not known it'. This absentmindedness, however, did not prevent Collins from being on the sharp lookout for any slights coming from the other direction and he was soon falling out with Gosse again over something Gosse had happened to say to him. Touchiness aside, however, Gosse and Collins were too suspicious of each other to get on well together for long. Gosse no doubt privately looked on Collins as an upstart, a possible rival and an intruder into the Swinburne circle (Gosse was always on the look out for likely competitors here), and Collins soon came to look on Gosse as a conceited and basically second-rate literary man, lacking the

classical education necessary to the true scholar while attempting
to impose on an all too gullible literary world.

4

Collins meanwhile was working hard on his own account to make
some impression as a scholar and critic. Editions apart—and the
Tourneur was soon followed by the *Poems of Lord Herbert of Cherbury*
in 1881 (also dubbed a very careless edition by a later editor in
1923)[24]—he was now producing a number of literary articles. His
first article on 'Aulus Gellius', a Roman collector of anecdotes of
famous men (a Churton Collins of his time?), was accepted by
Leslie Stephen for the *Cornhill* in 1878 and this was followed in
May the same year by an article on Dryden which Dr Smith
accepted for the *Quarterly Review*. This Dryden article was something of a breakthrough for Collins; Gosse praised it in the *Saturday
Review* in November 1878 and it later reappeared in Collins' *Essays
and Studies* (1895) where it received further praise from Saintsbury
as 'not merely one of the best things Mr Collins has done, but one
of the best on the subject; one certainly not to be missed by
anybody who is studying that subject'.[25]

By 1880, with further articles in preparation, Collins felt he was
making some mark in the literary world and on 20 February
recorded the following comment in his notebook:

> Had to-day, Saturday, Feb 20th 1880, an interview with Septimus
> Rivington, the publisher—he was very keen for me to write a work
> for them. Offered £200 down and royalty for a History of Queen
> Anne's Reign to be in three or four volumes. Offered to publish any
> other book of mine and *take the risk*. I am getting on I think.[26]

A year later he was dining with Dr Smith, editor of the *Quarterly*,
and keeping distinguished company:

> there were present the Earl of Derby, Courthope, Robert Brown-
> ing, Lord John Manners, Lady Manners, Lord something (not
> Odo) Russell, and others. Lord Derby spoke to me in very
> complimentary terms of my articles—so did Lord Manners, to all
> of whom I was specially introduced.[27]

Collins also met and cultivated Mark Pattison, Rector of Lincoln

College, Oxford, and a scholar of the severe sort that Collins admired. Collins first met Pattison in May 1880, when they talked of such things as the credibility of ancient history, Tacitus, the rise of Deism in England and Scaliger. Collins found him 'a very pleasant and most learned and kindly, scholarly soul'.[28] A correspondence was started—Collins of course called Pattison 'master'—and a series of literary topics touched on. Pattison, who had no liking for Jowett, responded warmly to Collins' freshness and enthusiasm which he found surprising in a Balliol graduate—as he told Collins,

> nothing is more inspiring than the enthusiasm of the young. You are especially happy considering you were at Balliol in having escaped without catching the Oxford superiority airs, and preserving to your age the power of admiration, and therefore of enjoyment of poetry.[29]

Pattison died in 1884 but always remained for Collins the best kind of literary scholar upholding the highest and most exacting standards. It was Pattison after all who advised someone who proposed editing Selden's Table Talk to proceed with the most strenuous and time-consuming rigour:

> The preparation was to be, first, to get the contents practically by heart, then to read the whole of the printed literature of Selden's day, and of the generation before him. In twenty years he promised me I should be prepared for the work.[30]

Collins himself as a literary scholar never got down to this sort of Casaubon-like preparation of the topic in hand, but he admired it as an ideal and when he wrote his scathing reviews of shoddily prepared works of literary scholarship clearly had it in mind.

Collins' delight in meeting famous men also brought him into contact with Browning again. He met Browning in March 1881 and this time—no longer the callow undergraduate—was not particularly impressed:

> With Browning I was miserably disappointed; there was a marked *vulgarity* about him, particularly in his accent and in the tone of his voice, & a certain indescribable savour of *sycophancy* of a man eager to be of a grade to which he did not belong; but the poet was

there—the poet's keen eye—the poet's heart—obvious in his remarks and descriptions: a sad, very thoughtful face, a great weight of thought over the eyes—for the rest a commonplace face and a very commonplace manner, in the brow and the eye only sat genius . . .[31]

Although disappointed that Browning did not come fully up to expectations (a poetic genius after all ought to look like a genius), Collins was keen to cultivate his acquaintance and in between meetings with Swinburne and others arranged at least one other meeting with the poet. Among other things close to Collins' concerns, they talked about the truth of Christianity and the possibility of a future state. Again Browning was disappointing: 'Vigorous common sense was the characteristic of his conversation—he literally said nothing which would be new to a person of any reflection.'[32] Browning obviously had nothing of Carlyle's force and originality and nothing of Swinburne's many-sided qualities which compelled Collins' affection whatever the growing differences between them. A meeting with Browning left Collins feeling flat; a meeting with Swinburne was more like the exciting encounter a meeting with a poetic genius should be. The lift Swinburne gave to Collins' feelings is well described in the following report Collins made of a walk with the poet over Putney Heath:

> In the afternoon we went for a walk over Putney Heath through Wimbledon: we stood for a time rapturously gazing at the scene from near the Church down on to the valley beneath—a heavenly piece of English scenery, he thought it as fine as anything he knew in England. We talked incessantly: about the influence of scenery on the emotions . . . We talked of Horace, Tasso, Virgil, Catullus, Tennyson, Browning . . . We had a most delightful walk—what a really sweet character he is, a most lovable human soul, so generous, so sympathetic, so noble.[33]

Fresh air, fine scenery, talking of literature with a great poet—this for Collins was the greatest of delights, a measure of his getting on as a literary man, and a joyful release from the grind of examination coaching and article writing.

5

In the early 1880s, as part of his plan to get on, Collins began to write more substantial pieces of literary history, biography and criticism. He wrote three articles on Tennyson for the *Cornhill* in January and July 1880 and July 1881 (later turned into a book *Illustrations of Tennyson*, 1891); three on Bolingbroke for the *Quarterly Review* in January 1880, January 1881 and April 1881; and two on Voltaire for the *Cornhill* in October and December 1882. The articles on Bolingbroke and Voltaire were turned into a book *Bolingbroke and Voltaire in England*, published by John Murray in 1886, and this represents his first attempt at a major contribution to literary history and biography.

Collins' book followed what became the characteristic Collinsian procedures in work of this kind: he took immediate issue with previous writers on the subject, dealt with new material to hand, and then offered his own strong and decisive judgments. He began by sharply exposing the faults of previous editors and biographers of Bolingbroke:

> The edition of his works by Mallet is, if we except the type and paper, one of the worst editions of an English author that ever issued from the press. It is frequently disfigured by misprints; it swarms with errors in punctuation; its text, as a very cursory collation with the original manuscripts will suffice to show, is not always to be depended on.[34]

Collins no doubt was not the man to lecture other editors on their shortcomings—however. He was also critical of Bolingbroke's previous biographers. George Wingrove Cooke's work was 'too superficial and too inaccurate to be ever likely to attain a permanent place in literature', and Thomas Macknight's 'Life', though diligent and impartial, was overlong, tedious and slipshod in style; even worse he said nothing about 'one of the most curiously interesting periods in his hero's career—the period between 1733 and 1736'. Collins it was understood was going to offer a much crisper account of Bolingbroke's career and attend to periods previous writers had neglected.

What follows is a cogent retailing of facts and incidents, carefully assembled from the available sources and an investigation of Bolingbroke's relationship with writers like Pope and Voltaire. Here Collins felt he was adding something to what was already known on the subject—for example, he finds considerably more borrowings by Pope from Bolingbroke in the *Essay on Man* than previous editors had noticed,[35] and goes more thoroughly than previous biographers into the question of Bolingbroke's relationship with Voltaire: 'it is a question which has never, in our opinion, received half the attention it deserves'. According to Collins, Voltaire's debt to Bolingbroke was immense:

> This will be at once evident if we compare what Voltaire has written on metaphysics, on early Christianity, on theological dogma, on the nature of the Deity, on inspiration, on religious sectarianism, on the authenticity of the Hebrew scriptures, on the authenticity of the gospels, on the credibility of profane historians, on the origin of civil society, on the origin of evil, on the study and true use of history—with what Bolingbroke has written on the same subjects.[36]

Collins had his own way of asserting his own views and refusing qualifications, but he certainly read up all his sources on this topic and supported his claims with a detailed list of texts by Bolingbroke and Voltaire which make for comparison.

The 'Voltaire' section of the book deals with 'an unwritten chapter in the literary history of the eighteenth century'. Voltaire was in England from 1726 until 1729 and his stay 'left its traces on almost everything which he subsequently produced, either as the professed disciple and interpreter of English teachers, or as an independent inquirer. It penetrated his life.'[37] Since this was an area largely neglected by other commentators, Collins spends some time discussing the specific English influences on Voltaire—very oddly, though, he makes no reference to John Morley's contribution to this topic in his *Voltaire* (1872).

Collins' book was an attempt to establish his own credentials as a biographer and to strike out some new territory for himself in the field of comparative literary studies. He later expanded his study of the literary relations between England and France into a further book—*Voltaire, Montesquieu and Rousseau in England* (1908)—and always intended to carry out further research into the question of literary connexions and influences when time permitted. He never found the time to get far with this, but a good proportion of his writings deals with comparative issues—something his wide reading in English, Greek, Latin, French and Italian literature equipped him to do—and when he came to consider the matter of literary syllabuses, he always gave supreme importance to the idea of 'influence'.

For readers at the time, however, Collins' book was chiefly noticed for its striking portrait of Bolingbroke. Collins, like many Victorian critics, had a certain distaste for the aristocratic sceptics of the eighteenth century but he drew Bolingbroke's attributes with some stylish touches—for example:

> Seldom has it been the lot even of the great leaders of mankind to unite in the same dazzling combination such an array of eminent qualities as met in this unhappy statesman. His intellect was of the highest and rarest order—keen, clear, logical, comprehensive, rapidly assimilative, inexhaustibly fertile. His memory was so prodigious that he complained, like Themistocles, of its indiscriminating tenacity; but the treasures of Bolingbroke's memory were at the ready call of a swift and lively intelligence ... His face and figure were such as sculptors love to dwell on; and such as more than one of his contemporaries have paused to describe. His person was tall and commanding; his features were of classical beauty, but eager, mobile, animated; his forehead was high and intellectual, his lips indicated eloquence, his eyes were full of fire. Grace and dignity blended themselves in his deportment ...[38]

And so on, and so on, for several more pages, together with a counterpointing of Bolingbroke's vices—his impetuosity, intemperance, egotism and cynicism. It all amounted not simply to an arresting portrait of Bolingbroke but to a piece of rhetorical virtuosity on Collins's part—the equivalent in writing to his brilliant feats of recitation.

The master of this mode of literary portraiture, of course, was Macaulay and there was much in Collins' approach and style—his forceful emphases and calculated balances—to remind contemporary readers of Macaulay. For some indeed it had Macaulay's faults of overstatement and assertion. The reviewer in the *Pall Mall Gazette*, for example, wrote: 'In calling Mr Churton Collins "a new Macaulay" we intend both praise and censure. The essays now before us are at once vigorous and irritating.'[39] This tended to become the standard verdict on most of Collins' writings as time passed. More open praise came, of course, from Swinburne, who was still anxious to flatter and encourage him; Swinburne found the Bolingbroke portrait quite brilliant: 'Macaulay could not have made a more vivid and striking figure of him.'[40]

From this time forward, frequent comparisons were made between Collins and Macaulay, which Collins clearly delighted in. According to Frank Harris, for whom Collins later worked on the *Saturday Review*, Collins worshipped Macaulay: 'He admired Macaulay beyond reason, knew pages of him by heart; thought him very unjustly treated by Arnold; was delighted at being compared with him. "Macaulay", he declared, "was one of the great English writers." '[41] No doubt he worked hard to catch Macaulay's tricks and flourishes, but Collins at times also found Macaulay's influence daunting and felt that he was being over-powered by it. In a moment of depression in August 1884, he felt that all he was producing in his writing was 'a wretched parody of Macaulay',[42] and he was much relieved when he was told by J. A. Froude, the historian and biographer of Carlyle, that his style was really his own 'and not imitated from anyone'.[43] Whether this was true or not, the literary world in 1886 was talking about a new Macaulay and everyone was aware of a new vigorous voice on the scene. Collins had emerged as a learned and assertive historian and critic, someone prepared to state his own opinions with clarity and force and eager to challenge contrary views with uncomfortable directness.

NOTES

1 See John Gross, *The Rise and Fall of the Man of Letters*, 1969, pp. 132 ff. and 158 ff.
2 L. C. Collins, op. cit. p. 22 says that Collins' first *Globe* article appeared on 18 December 1872, but 3 August is the date of his first fee in the Notebooks.
3 *Edgbastonia*, March 1906, p. 48.
4 L. C. Collins, op. cit., pp. 189 ff.
5 Ibid., p. 214.
6 Ibid., p. 25.
7 See for example J. C. Collins, 'The New Scheme for The Indian Civil

Service Examinations', *The Contemporary Review*, LIX, June 1891, pp. 836–51.

8   L. C. Collins, op. cit., p. 25.

9   Collins' two letters to Carlyle dated 1874 and 26 September 1875 are in the National Library of Scotland.

10 This was one of the ways Gosse for example advanced his career; see Rupert Croft-Cooke, *Feasting with Panthers*, 1967, p. 85.

11 L. C. Collins, op. cit., p. 46.

12 Ibid., p. 29.

13 Collins to W. Blackwood, MS letter, 4 December 1874. Collins' twenty letters to the publishers Blackwood are in the National Library of Scotland.

14 This letter from Swinburne to Collins is dated 14 October 1873 by L. C. Collins, op. cit., p. 26, but 14 October 1874 by Cecil Y. Lang, *The Swinburne Letters*, 6 vols., New Haven, 1959, II, 342.

15 *Swinburne Letters*, III, 229.

16 Irving Ribner (ed.), *The Atheist's Tragedy*, Methuen,1964, p. xxix.

17 T. S. Eliot, *Selected Essays*, 1951, p. 189.

18 *Swinburne Letters*, III, 22.

19 L. C. Collins, op. cit., pp.39–40.

20 Ibid., p. 49.

21 *Swinburne Letters*, V, 146–47.

22 The standard account of Gosse by E. Charteris, *The Life and Letters of Sir Edmund Gosse*, 1931, has recently been superseded by Ann Thwaite's *Edmund Gosse: A Literary Landscape 1849–1928*, 1984.

23 Five surviving letters from Collins to Gosse are in the Brotherton Library, University of Leeds.

24 See the *Poems of Edward Lord Herbert*, ed. G. C. Moore Smith, Oxford, 1923, p. xxviii.

25 *The Bookman*, March 1895, p. 179.

26 L. C. Collins, op. cit., p. 38.

27 Ibid., p. 47.

28 Ibid., p. 41.

29 Ibid., p. 75.

30 'Anecdotes about the late Mark Pattison', *Pall Mall Gazette*, 28 May 1885, p. 11.

31 L. C. Collins, op. cit., p. 48.

32 Ibid., p. 83.

33 Ibid., p. 52.

34 *Bolingbroke and Voltaire in England*, 1886, p. 3.

35 Ibid., p. 192.

36   Ibid., p. 142.
37   Ibid., p. 227.
38   Ibid., pp. 6–8.
39   *Pall Mall Gazette*, 24 June 1886, p. 4.
40   *Swinburne Letters*, V, 146.
41   Frank Harris, *Latest Contemporary Portraits*, New York, 1927, p. 314.
42   J. C. Collins, Notebooks, 6 August 1884.
43   L. C. Collins, op. cit., p.87.

CHAPTER THREE

UNIVERSITY EXTENSION LECTURING

At some unrecorded time in the 1870s, Collins met Pauline Mary Strangways, only daughter of Thomas Henry Strangways, and what followed is still not fully clear. The gist of it, however, is that their first child (L. C. Collins) was born in January 1878 while they were still unmarried, the marriage not taking place for some reason until April (See Appendix 1). What this meant for Collins in terms of guilt and embarrassment can only be guessed at but it certainly brought him under new financial pressures since Laurence Churton Collins was simply the first of seven children. L. C. Collins makes only passing reference to his mother in his book and says nothing about when or where his father first met her. But from what he does say, and from odd notes in Collins' notebooks, she was evidently a sweet-natured, long-suffering woman, who managed to cope well with Collins' moods and depression and with the normally uncertain state of their finances. Collins in turn, despite all his worries, doubts and probably guilt, obviously returned her love and told his children 'You have had the best mother that children could ever have and I the best wife a man ever had.'[1] Whenever he felt he had treated her badly he always brooded over it for days, jotting down thoughts on the plight of women in general: one of the attractions of Robert Greene's 'novels' for Collins was the sharp contrast drawn in them between 'the purity and long-suffering of women, and the follies and selfishness of men'.[2]

2

With new domestic responsibilities and money problems, Collins would have found it hard to get by, but luckily he managed to find extra work as a University Extension lecturer from 1880 on—probably thanks to Scoones' recommendation. The Extension Movement began in the 1860s in response both to an appeal for adult education classes on the part of various organizations—working men's societies, women's associations and the like—and to a growing conviction in the universities themselves that something should be done by way of extending educational opportunities beyond the confines of Oxford, Cambridge and London.[3] The Movement started in a piecemeal, unofficial way thanks to the enterprise of particular university lecturers—men like James Stuart of Cambridge—who organized lectures and classes by invitation up and down the country, but during the 1870s this unofficial work was put on an official basis by the universities as an organized University Extension scheme. Cambridge was first in the field in 1873, followed by London in 1876, followed by Oxford in 1878, and by 1889 there were more than 22,000 students attending some 200 courses.[4] By this time, of all the subjects offered, English literature was certainly the most popular: out of 104 courses offered by the London Society for the Extension of University Teaching in 1889, 25 were on English literature, far more than on any other subject.[5]

If the Extension Movement offered new opportunities for adults to take up educational interests, it also of course offered new opportunities for young graduates who were either unemployed or looking for supplementary sources of income. For someone like Collins, Extension teaching was a godsend; it gave him a more or less regular income and tapped his missionary enthusiasm for teaching and spreading the cultural word through the nation. True he had no formal qualifications for teaching English literature (one of his later arguments for a School of English at Oxford was that it would provide qualified teachers for the Extension Movement) but he had been teaching the subject for six years at Scoones' and was clearly something better than the average crammer. Besides, none of the literature lecturers at this time had any qualifications in English: most were graduates in History or Classics who came to English literature through their own interest in the subject; though self-taught they were often men of wide culture with a thorough knowledge of ancient and modern literatures. What they lacked in terms of special expertise in particular areas of English studies, they made up for with their range of literary knowledge and, above all, with their quasi-religious sense of cultural mission. Men like Henry Morley, R. G. Moulton and Collins himself with their learning, their belief in the value of the subject and their teaching skills seemed not to be unduly handicapped by the lack of formal qualifications in the subject.

The lecture course was the centrepiece of Extension work and many Extension students attended simply to hear a good speaker. But a varying number also stayed for the class discussions which followed the lecture, wrote weekly essays and took the terminal examination for which a certificate was awarded. At Collins' lectures at Croydon in 1882, for example, out of a regular attendance of about fifty for the lectures, about 30 usually attended the classes and some 20 essays were produced weekly.[6] The examinations attracted fewer students: during the 1881–82 session, for example, out of 394 students taking English courses in 4 London centres, a mere 43 took the examinations.[7]

The London Society for the Extension of University Teaching[8] had been in operation for almost four years when Collins joined it in 1880. For the first two years there were no courses on English literature, though History, Political Economy, Logic, Physics, Geology and Physiology were offered. The first course on English literature was given by Edward Arber of University College London—and later one of Collins' predecessors in the chair of English at Birmingham University. A year later, in October 1879, four lecturers, W. R. Morfill, J. W. Hales, E. P. Scrymgour and A. Ainger, were giving courses on various periods of literature and English was gaining a rapid popularity. Collins' first courses (for which he was paid £30 per course) began in January 1880 at centres in Wimbledon, Brixton and Tower Hamlets.[9] Financial needs meant that he took on too many courses over the years (upwards of 3000 lectures in all according to L. C. Collins)[10] and the strain of incessant teaching, travelling and marking inevitably weighed him down at times. All the same Collins found his true metier in Extension teaching, where he could instruct, inspire and parade his vast knowledge of literature before crowds of admiring students, and despite the strain of it all he was always eager to take on further courses at new centres. During his twenty-seven years with the London Society he lectured at more than seventy different centres.

Collins typically was soon into the swing of Extension work. In the 1880–81 session he gave four courses (three on Shakespeare and one on Milton); the following season he gave five (two simply called 'English literature', one on the period 1793–1840, one on Shakespeare, and one on the period 1509–1625). Two years later, he was giving twelve courses (five on Shakespeare, five on 'English Poetry' and two on the 'Age of Pope'); in fact apart from two courses on Shakespeare that session, Collins gave all the London Society courses in English literature.[11] The range of his work also increased rapidly over this period. At some centres consecutive courses were organized in the interests of continuous study—students took a series of courses from, say, Chaucer down to the Victorians in chronological sequence—and Collins took a major part in this work. The Council in reporting on the 1883 session, for example, remarked that 'Mr J. C. Collins is now delivering a fifth consecutive course of lectures at Croydon, which will conclude a critical survey of English literature from the Elizabethan era to the present day ... At the Camden Road centre the same lecturer delivered last term the fourth of a series of courses covering much the same ground.'[12]

Collins' approach to the teaching of literature was a mixture of the enthusiastic, the earnest and the systematic. His memory for facts and quotations was such that he was able to speak without notes for much of the time and, according to all reports, his lectures always had an 'air of ease and spontaneity'.[13] A typical letter from one of his former students reads as follows:

> My gratitude to you is very deep, for you have that rare gift of imparting some of your wonderful stores of knowledge so as to enrich your hearers. Instead of feeling my own want of education more keenly, you draw out all that I possess and at the end of each lecture give some magic oil to keep alive the feeble flame at home.[14]

Collins, of course, must have met some unreceptive classes or had his off days, but judging from the comments provided by his students he was an unflagging and inspiring teacher and once on stage forgot all his worries and problems in his delight for the subject in hand. For the keen student—someone like Gissing's Gilbert Grail who 'loved literature passionately' and who 'hungered to know the history of man's mind through all the ages'[15]— Collins was the ideal teacher, encouraging, learned, kindly and sympathetic; a very different figure from the hectoring critic of the journals and reviews.

Extension teaching, however, was not just a matter of inspired readings from great authors; there were also the more academic sides of literary study to consider—the question of background, conventions and influences, all of which, of course, Collins was well versed in and keen to discuss. In a pamphlet called *Hints for the Systematic Study of Elizabethan Literature* (1888),[16] designed for the benefit of Home Reading Societies, Collins set out his ideas for this thorough-going study of English literature. Students were told that they had to consider literature from both the historical and the critical sides. So far as the first was concerned, they needed to get a clear view of the political, social, moral and intellectual conditions under which the literature of all periods developed; to see its relationship with literature of earlier and later periods; to see the nature and extent of influences on it by the literature of other nations; and finally to get a clear sense of the different epochs into which literature could be divided. The critical side was of course the study of particular works and the business of interpretation and evaluation, which, as Collins insisted, must be a matter of critical argument and not vague impressionism.

If all this sounds absurdly ambitious and of doubtful value for Extension students, such historical approaches were the established mode of the day. English literary historians like Henry Morley and W. J. Courthope were less dogmatic on the issue of historical determinism than their French counterparts, Taine and Brunetière, but they were nonetheless keen to examine literature in terms of epochs, evolution, race, milieu and moment.[17] Collins too was caught up in this enthusiasm for historical study and in an article entitled 'Can English Literature be Taught?' written in 1887 argued the need to see literature as an 'organic whole', as 'the expression of national idiosyncrasies revealing themselves under various conditions', and as the creation of particular individuals living in particular epochs.[18] This sounds deterministic enough but, like his heroes Sainte-Beuve and Matthew Arnold, Collins was more flexible in his attitude when it came to teaching and writing criticism; a special case could always be made out for the literary genius who rose above his conditions and epoch. In the event, he tended to dispense with strict theories and settled for sound knowledge of particular periods.

A good idea of Collins' teaching approach can be had from the syllabuses which he, like all Extension lecturers, had to prepare beforehand both for the benefit of his students and as an indication to the supervisory body—the Universities Joint Board—of the worthwhileness of the course. The following was prepared for a course on 'Shakespeare and his Age' which he gave at the Wimbledon centre between November 1880 and February 1881:[19]

Lecture I. The Elizabethan Age, its limits—the causes which conspired to form it. Its essential characteristics—various influences operating on it, Greek, Roman, Italian. Principal contemporaries of Shakespeare in prose and verse.

Lecture II. History of Drama up to Shakespeare. Stage History 1562–82.

Lecture III. Principal dramatists preceding Shakespeare. Their lives sketched—works discussed—influence on Shakespeare's genius estimated.

Lecture IV. Principal contemporary dramatists of Shakespeare discussed and enumerated.

Lecture V. Biography of Shakespeare—sources for this life—contemporary notices of him—is there an autobiographical element in his writing?

Lecture VI. His poems discussed—their characteristics—various theories about the sonnets—most probable solution of the mystery—the sonnet discussed—various classes of the sonnet—class to which Shakespeare's belong.

Lecture VII. Various stages in Shakespeare's work—how far and in what way they are distinctly marked—what principles must guide us in assigning the period of the composition of his plays—early period described and the plays of it enumerated and discussed—authorship of the three parts of Henry VI, extent of Shakespeare's share in them.

Lecture VIII. Second period—characteristics of work produced then—plays comprised in it enumerated and discussed—characteristic passages selected for illustration—the world they describe, the characters they depict.

Lecture IX.   The third period—its characteristics—plays comprised in it discussed at length; Lear, Othello, Macbeth.

Lecture X.   Same subject continued; Timon of Athens, Antony and Cleopatra, Troilus and Cressida, Measure for Measure, Coriolanus discussed.

Lecture XI.   The last period—plays comprising it discussed—the doubtful plays.

Lecture XII.   Distinctive features of Shakespeare's genius—comparison with Homer, Chaucer and the Greek dramatists. History of Shakespearian criticism, principal Shakespearian critics discussed. Conclusion.

Like all systematic approaches to literature, this seems a long way removed from the notion of uplift and inspiration talked of by Carlyle and Arnold—and of course by Collins himself—in their comments on the subject. Once it was packaged into a syllabus, literature looked much less alluring. Despite this fact of life, we know from reports that Collins' lecture talks were always lively and interesting. In the case of Shakespeare, along with the basic information, he would have entertained his class with scathing comments on critics who speculated too wildly about such things as the autobiographical element in the plays, the mystery of W.H. and the dark lady, and the theory that Bacon was the real author of the plays—these are all topics which recur in Collins' critical writings.[20] And if the lectures as outlined suggest that Shakespeare was only skimmed, it needs to be remembered that the lectures were followed up by a variety of activities—play readings, class discussion of particular points, private reading and essay writing.

Collins was also a demanding teacher when it came to extra study. At Croydon in 1883, for example, when dealing with Wordsworth he gave the class 'a short sketch of the Platonic philosophy and exhorted them to read attentively a translation of the Phaedo'. His students responded to this exhortation, circulated the Phaedo round the class, and showed in their essays that they had grasped its theme.[21] This, however, was at the top end of the

Extension world: Croydon as a predominantly middle-class centre was a special case. Elsewhere, where the class was less keen or less literate, the standard was obviously lower. At Cheltenham in 1887, for example, when Collins was teaching a Shakespeare course for the Oxford University Extension Committee, the results were more humdrum. Of the 31 candidates who took the examination, the examiner, F. S. Pulling, wrote: 'It is very clear that the lectures have been carefully listened [to] and that notes have been diligently taken, but there is little evidence of individual and independent thought or of much reading beyond the most elementary text-books.'[22] Along with the real success stories of the Extension Movement—of which Collins had his large share—there were also less exciting things to report.

Whatever the general standard of Extension classes— and the best students tended not to take the examinations—Collins was a keen innovator as well as a capable teacher. Despite the fact that his subject was English literature only, this did not prevent him from relating it to other literatures and from constantly emphasizing the classical influence. He was also keen to set up beginners courses in Classics for Extension students and wrote in 1889: 'Nothing indeed is more common than to hear the more advanced members of the classes complaining that their ignorance of classical literature is a great misfortune to them, and that the more they advance in their study of English literature the more they feel impeded by their ignorance of classical literature.'[23] For Collins, English literature, important though it was, was merely one department of European literature which also included classical and other modern literatures. A full and proper understanding of it therefore involved a consideration of its wider relationships.

With R. G. Moulton and others, Collins took a leading part in the development of classical courses in Extension centres during the 1890s. By July 1894 in fact eight centres were offering classical instruction and the same summer Collins was in Oxford giving a course of twelve lectures on the 'Homeric Age' designed to form 'a popular introduction to the study of Greek literature'. By this time, of course, he was a well-known figure of the Extension Movement, one of its best lecturers and a successful promoter of its interests on the literary side. He was always in demand to give Extension addresses, chair meetings and set out the importance of the study of literature for the public at large. Chairing an Extension Conference at Oxford in 1892, for example, he outlined the aesthetic, ethical and political benefits of literary study in a way which brought the ideals of Jowett and Arnold directly to the public, and in May the same year told the students of Gresham College that the best remedy for the characteristic vices of the Victorian age was the study of Greek literature. For the Extension Movement itself, Collins was the teacher 'who has done more than any other single man to awaken and nourish throughout the Metropolitan centres an interest in the new Humanist Revival which is now a growing force in our midst'.[24]

3

By the early 1890s, then, Collins could be well satisfied with his progress on the Extension front. He was successful enough in fact to consider moving on to something higher, and better paid, in the educational field. If he had a blind-spot it was in the area of Anglo-Saxon, then well-established as the respectable academic basis for English as a university examination subject. Collins, like many literary men brought up on the Classics, had an arrogant contempt for Anglo-Saxon literature seeing it as, at best, merely the primitive forerunner of a literature that only matured later under the civilizing influence of Classical literature. He therefore strongly objected to the priority given to Anglo-Saxon in university English syllabuses. 'It is nothing short of criminal', he remarked on one occasion, 'for our educational legislators to insist on that time and energy being frittered on the barren drudgery of acquiring a smattering of Anglo-Saxon, Early English, and the like, which might be devoted to the study of this, the parent and Master Literature of the world.'[25] The parent and Master Literature was of course Greek. Since Collins was always eager to give forth on this topic, he soon established a reputation as a violent opponent of Anglo-Saxon and Philology which for several years, until he softened his tone, blighted his chances of getting an English post in a university.

So far as the Extension Movement was concerned, however, Collins' literary preferences were totally acceptable; here the emphasis was firmly on literature not philology (mainly Shakespeare and later literature), and the Extension lecturers liked to see themselves fulfilling responsibilities towards modern literature and the cause of humane education which most universities ignored. As R. G. Moulton put it in 1890:

> University Extension lecturers are going up and down the country and are showing the universities, as John Wesley showed the sleeping Church, that there is a world outside their charmed circle which is being influenced and moulded by that which they regard so lightly—literature.[26]

Collins obviously enough delighted in taking a leading role in this literary-humanist-evangelical movement.

Yet, equally obviously, there were times when he felt that he ought to move out of the Extension world to improve his own financial position and status and to give himself more time to research and write. Extension teaching was back-breaking work and Collins also worked at an exhausting pace: some weeks he gave as many as twenty lectures in different centres, schools and private houses, frequently offering as many as four or even five in a single day. He also had to mark dozens of essays every week and in 1890 was granted the aid of an assistant marker by the Extension authorities.[27] On top of all this of course came his coaching work at Scoones' (until 1888) and his articles, books and reviews. Since his indolent Oxford days, Collins had transformed himself into a demonic worker, enjoying all he did, but also feeling the constant need to seek extra work to earn enough to give his growing family a decent standard of living. As early as 1883, writing of the completion of his Swift article in his notebook, Collins indicates the strains and stresses of his mode of life:

> Sent off this day, Monday June 17th 1883, the article finished thank God at last; it has been produced in the mere by-moments of a life full of an almost incredible amount of work. I think I have earned upwards of £800 every shilling by sheer work since the thing was begun. I am very depressed about it.[28]

He was already making a name for himself as a literary historian and critic—someone to mention in the same breath with the likes of, say, Symonds and Gosse—and he might yet produce some books of lasting merit, but not if he had to put all his energies into

Extension work. There were times when Collins worried whether he could survive the pace he had to set himself.

Then, early in 1885, a highly attractive offer presented itself. A new chair of English Language and Literature—The Merton Chair—was set up at Oxford and applications invited. The brief was that 'The Merton Professor of English Language and Literature shall lecture and give instruction on the history and criticism of the English Language and Literature, and on the works of approved English authors.' Collins, with his eye on the last part of this rather than the rest, immediately sent off his application for the post. His notebook entries of this time show him to be weighed down by depression and overwork; on 26 April he wrote 'My mind is I know in a fearfully morbid state & as I was told today I am a burden to everybody as well as to myself.'[29] This state of mind which was clearly causing frictions in the Collins household, no doubt prompted him to think of alternatives to his present career. In any case the Oxford post was an extremely attractive proposition; it was very well paid—£900 p.a.—much more than Collins was earning by hard labour in the Extension field and it required the Professor to give only forty-two lectures per year—at Collins' rate of work about a fortnight's load, though, of course, something more substantial would be required from the Merton Professor. Other considerations apart, the Professor would be able to play a leading part in establishing English studies in the University. As an Oxford man and as an ambitious and successful teacher, Collins would clearly relish the openings in this area.

Collins was also no doubt encouraged by Gosse's recent success as Clark Lecturer in English Literature at Cambridge. The Clark Lectures, established in 1878 by W. G. Clark, one of the editors of the Cambridge Shakespeare, were something like the equivalent of the lectures given at Oxford by the Professor of Poetry. Gosse's lectures on English literature from Shakespeare to Pope had been very well received at Cambridge and were about to be published in book form by the University Press. Collins, whose relationship with Gosse was quite distant and cool by this time, no doubt thought himself Gosse's superior both as a teacher and as a scholar and felt that if Cambridge could appoint a Gosse, Oxford could certainly appoint a Collins. Admittedly he had taken a mediocre degree from Oxford, but since 1872 he had redeemed himself by hard work; besides Gosse had no degree at all. All these considerations must have gone through Collins' mind when he wrote out his application for the chair.

Judging by his letter of application,[30] Collins was keen to play down the language side of the post—the 'Merton Professorship of English *Literature*', as he styled it. He said that he was an experienced lecturer and writer on the subject of English literature and that he had been 'a voluminous contributor to periodical literature'. Testimonials were provided by G. J. Goschen, President of the London Society for the Extension of University Teaching, and by W. B. Scoones. Both spoke for his excellent abilities as a teacher of literature. Leslie Stephen (former editor of the *Cornhill*) and William Smith (editor of the *Quarterly Review*) guaranteed his wide knowledge of literature. Goschen was enthusiastic about his Extension work: 'wherever a new centre has been formed, Council has felt peculiar confidence in sending Mr Collins to lecture there, and wherever he has lectured once he has been asked to lecture again'. Scoones supported this and stressed—with the Merton Post in mind—that it had been 'among university men that Mr Churton Collins' very pronounced qualifications as a lecturer have developed'. Both Stephen and Smith, as editors of leading journals who had published Collins' work, spoke up for his ability to investigate literary topics with great skill and praised him as a critic and reviewer.

The news that Oxford was to appoint a Professor of English Language *and* Literature created immense interest and argument in April 1885. A number of literary men—including Gosse, Dowden, Saintsbury and A. C. Bradley, apart from Collins himself[31]—applied for the post but there were also other candidates, including A. S. Napier and Henry Sweet (the Oxford philologist and author of the famous *Anglo-Saxon Reader*) whose interests were more linguistic than literary. Arguments about what kind of a Professor—literary man or philologist—ought to get the chair took place on all sides as the date for the election drew near. In the *Academy* for example Walter Skeat, Professor of Anglo-Saxon at Cambridge, pointed out the absurdity of asking the new Professor to be an expert in both language and literature: 'If any such phoenix exists, he must certainly be worth £900 per annum.'[32] Henry Sweet agreed, but went further in insisting that the real need was for a language specialist (presumably someone like himself) not a dilettante literary man: 'it is hardly worth paying £900 a year for the privilege of hearing some clever literary man read aloud his magazine articles before he sends them to press'.[33] The tone was already getting rancorous. The *Oxford Magazine*, however, disagreed with the language men, deplored the muddle that had developed, and insisted that the post 'ought to be associated with the names of none but the greatest English critics, and the greatest expositors of our literature'.[34] Unfortunately 'the greatest English critics' were uninterested in the whole affair—though rumours circulated in the *Oxford Magazine* that Matthew Arnold might have been approached.

In the event, at the end of May, Oxford ended further speculation by appointing a philologist, A. S. Napier, to the chair, thereby inviting further controversy. Napier's interests were almost exclusively in Early English philology; he gained his doctorate at Göttingen in 1882 for a thesis on the works of Archbishop Wulfstan and had been Professor of English in the same university before returning to Oxford, where he had been an undergraduate. Napier's credentials were just right for a Professor of Philology, but as the *Oxford Magazine* put it the Merton Chair ought to have been a Chair of Literature not Philology.[35] This was certainly Collins' view of it. Bitterly disappointed by his own failure in the matter, he saw Napier's appointment as a victory for all those people he despised—philologists, Anglo-Saxonists, textual scholars, and the like—over the literary men, and from this time forward found a new mission as a campaigner for literary studies versus the pretensions of philology. L. C. Collins makes no mention of his father's application for the Merton Chair in his biography—not surprisingly perhaps, since the disappointment was something Collins never really lived down. The day he heard that he had been unsuccessful he wrote in his notebook, 'It would be impossible to conceive a state of more abject misery than I am in'[36]—failure meant, among other things, no relief from the non-stop demands of Extension teaching and the constant worries about money. All the same, rejection by Oxford gave Collins a new cause to fight for and put new vigour into his arguments for literature and literary education.

There can be no doubt that Collins was both over-optimistic

and naive in his application for the Oxford Chair. Even if the University had been looking for a literary man in 1885 there is no reason to suppose that they would have settled on Collins rather than any of the others. Collins had published respectable articles on English and classical literature and was known as a forceful critic and a good teacher but the other candidates could make equal claims. Ten years later he would have been able to make a stronger challenge for the post, but in 1885 he was only just coming into notice.

Collins' failure at Oxford in 1885 had its bitter sequel four years later when he tried again for a university chair, this time at University College London. Once again Collins was optimistic: after all he was even more experienced as a teacher and had further articles to his name. But again he was disappointed and the chair was given to W. P. Ker who had previously held the chair of English at the University College of South Wales. According to Henry Morley, who was one of his referees in later applications for university posts, Collins missed the London chair mainly because he had never been 'required to lecture upon Anglo-Saxon, or to give public evidence of his attention to the language studies that form a large part of the work required in preparation for the English Examinations at the University of London'.[37] This must have been even harder for Collins to swallow than his Oxford defeat—everywhere he turned he came up against the Anglo-Saxon barrier. Yet the incident once again shows how naive and maladroit Collins was when it came to making a career for himself. In January 1887 he had the following to say about philology and its practitioners:

> As an instrument of culture it ranks, in our opinion, very low indeed. It certainly contributes nothing to the cultivation of the taste. It as certainly contributes nothing to the education of the emotions. The mind it neither enlarges nor refines. On the contrary, it too often induces or confirms that peculiar woodenness and opacity of moral and intellectual vision, which has in all ages been characteristic of mere philologists, and of which we have appalling illustrations in such a work as Bentley's Milton.[38]

This put the philologists forcibly in their place and publicized once again Collins' utter contempt for philology (at least as an educational discipline)—a good honest comment. But why then, only two years later, did he apply for a chair of English in a university heavily committed to language studies? And why did he expect the university to take his application seriously? The answer is that Collins often said things in print as a deliberate provocation and was much less inflexible and unreasonable in practice than he sounded—no doubt he naively hoped appointments boards would realize this. He also confidently expected to be able to change any English courses in favour of literary interests if he ever got an appointment (he had to wait until 1904 for one). Meanwhile, however, his failures in 1885 and 1889 simply intensified his dislike of the philologists, and of the approaches to English at Oxford and London, and from this time forward he became the leading militant figure in the Literature versus Philology debate.

NOTES

1   L. C. Collins, op. cit., p. 132.
2   J. C. Collins, *Essays and Studies*, 1895, p. 168.
3   See Edwin Welch, *The Peripatetic University*, Cambridge, 1973, especially chapters 1 to 3.
4   *University Extension Journal*, 1 April 1890, p. 25.
5   Ibid., 1 March 1890, pp. v–vi.
6   London Society for the Extension of University Teaching: *Reports from Lecturers and Examiners* 1881–82, p.23.
7   London Society etc., *Report of the Council* for 1883, p. 14.
8   The London Society was not part of London University but included university representatives on its Council. See Welch op. cit., p. 85.
9   London Society etc., *Report of the Council* for 1880, Appx. 1.
10 L. C. Collins, op. cit., p. 61.
11 London Society etc., *Report of the Council* for 1884, Appx. II.
12 Ibid., 1883, p. 15.
13 L. C. Collins, op. cit., p. 63.
14 Ibid., p. 69.
15 George Gissing, *Thyrza*, 3 vols., 1887, I, 114.
16 This pamphlet is in the Bodleian Library.
17 René Wellek, *A History of Modern Criticism 1750–1950*, 5 vols., 1966 IV, 141 ff.
18 J. C. Collins, 'Can English Literature be Taught?', *Nineteenth Century*, XXII, November 1887, p. 648.

19 This and other of Collins' Extension syllabuses are in the Bodleian Library.

20 See for example Collins' reviews of books on Shakespeare in *Ephemera Critica*, 1901.

21 London Society etc., *Report of the Council* for 1883, p.14.

22 Oxford University Extension: *Lecturers' and Examiners' Reports* for 1886–87, p. 174.

23 J. C. Collins, 'The Universities in Contact with the People', *Nineteenth Century*, October 1889, p. 579.

24 *University Extension Journal*, 15 March 1893, p. 176.

25 Ibid., 15 June 1892, p. 82.

26 Ibid., 1 February 1890, p. 90.

27 London Society etc., *Minutes of the University Board*, 26 November 1890.

28 L. C. Collins, op. cit., p. 74.

29 Notebooks, 26 April 1885.

30 Collins' testimonials and application for the Merton Chair are in the Bodleian Library.

31 See D. J. Palmer, *The Rise of English Studies*, Oxford, 1965, p. 79.

32 The *Academy*, 18 April 1885, p. 275.

33 Ibid., 20 April 1885, p. 295. Henry Sweet was a peripheral figure throughout the Oxford English studies dispute. Having failed twice in applications for Oxford chairs, he was finally made Reader in Phonetics in 1901. He is said to be the original for Shaw's Professor Higgins in *Pygmalion*.

34 *Oxford Magazine*, 20 May 1885, p. 230.

35 Ibid., 10 June 1885, p. 281.

36 Notebooks, 28 May 1885.

37 Collins used Morley's reference in his application for the Oxford Chair of English Literature in 1904.

38 J. C. Collins, 'Petition addressed to the Hebdomadal Council for the Foundation of a School of Modern Literature', *Quarterly Review*, 164, January 1887, p. 265.

CHAPTER FOUR

THE SYMONDS AND GOSSE FRACAS

Collins' first leap into notoriety was taken in October 1885 with his review of John Addington Symonds' *Shakspere's Predecessors in the English Drama* (1884). This was followed in October 1886 by an even more scathing review of Gosse's *From Shakespeare to Pope: An Inquiry into the Causes and Phenomena of the Rise of Classical Poetry in England* (1885). In both cases, and particularly in the second, these reviews were seen as deliberate personal attacks on the writers concerned and they gave Collins his reputation as a murderous reviewer. Since, as time went by, he came to be remembered for the persecution of Symonds and Gosse rather than for anything else these reviews established him for all time as the 'louse on the locks of literature'—a phrase invented by Tennyson to comfort the distressed Gosse.[1] Collins certainly played his part in creating this image by his cutting sarcasm and ridicule but the whole episode needs to be seen in a fuller context than it has customarily been given. Collins' tone and manner were unfortunate and undoubtedly offensive but the books in question—Gosse's especially—had glaring faults which cried out for demolition. If Collins had preferred to go about this work in a cooler, Arnoldian fashion he would have been spared the embarrassment and notoriety which followed the publication of his articles.

Symonds[2] was already a well-established literary man in 1884 when his book on Shakespeare's predecessors appeared. At Balliol a few years before Collins arrived there, he had won the Newdigate Prize for Poetry and had taken a double first in Classics; after a spell as a Fellow of Magdalen, and a number of personal crises and problems discussed by his biographer, he launched into a career as a literary critic and historian with works on Greek, Italian and English literature. His best known work the *Renaissance in Italy* began to appear in several volumes from 1875 onwards but he had already published work on the Elizabethan dramatists in the 1860s. His *Shakspere's Predecessors in the English Drama*, begun in 1882, was an ambitious attempt to trace the evolutionary development of English drama from its crude origins to its maturity in Shakespeare. In this Symonds received strong encouragement from A. H. Bullen, who had already published reprints of Elizabethan literature and who was a recognized authority on the period. However, when the book appeared in 1884, Symonds himself was not really satisfied with it and reviewers were generally unenthusiastic. One of them wrote, 'there is nothing new in the book, nothing that has not already been as well or better said, nothing that makes it indispensable or even useful to the student who has already broken ground'.[3]

So it might have rested there but for Collins' devastating review which he began to write in April 1884. Collins had no personal knowledge of Symonds at the time and no reason to dislike him, but from his schooldays, as we have seen, he had a hyperactive conscience about literary standards and by 1884 considered himself an authority on literary topics. Where Elizabethan literature was concerned, he had taught Shakespeare to many Extension classes, had edited Tourneur, and had thoroughly studied the question of origins, influences and tendencies—the very issues Symonds had taken up in his book. If there was any personal element in the attack on Symonds, it might have been in the reflection that Symonds had written badly the kind of book that Collins himself—had he had Symonds's opportunities—would have written well.

Collins' review took him over a year to complete. He began it on 30 April 1884 and revised the proofs in October 1885; throughout this period he was struggling against acute depression in a way which makes reading his private notebook a disturbing experience. Collins suffered from periodic bouts of manic depression throughout his life; doctors put this down to overwork yet, oddly enough, though the depressions frequently brought his writing to a standstill, they seem never to have interrupted his teaching. L. C. Collins recalls how his father would sometimes set off to lecture feeling utterly wretched, yet within five minutes of starting the session would be totally absorbed in the subject and as lively and cheerful as ever. The depression, however, would immediately return when Collins was not fully occupied by his teaching, and would sometimes last for months on end.[4] As a teacher, Collins could lose himself in the topic under discussion; as a writer, anxious to make his mark with a learned and highly critical readership, he plainly had to assert himself against a recurring sense of possible failure.

2

The period 1884–85 was a particularly black time for Collins and his failure to get the Merton Professorship in April 1885 clearly exacerbated matters. Some brief extracts from his notebook—not referred to in L. C. Collins' book—show the state he was sinking to:

> 6 August 1884.   A day of incessant labour—the miserable result one sentence.

> 20 August 1884.   Returned this evening from a week's visit to Oxford—wrote almost four pages of my article then. The change has made me another man—feel contented and hopeful now.

> 21 March 1885.   I am now in the middle of my ordinary work so that I have very little time for doing my article, i.e. pre Shakespearian Drama which has been virtually disconti-nued since last Autumn ... I am very depressed, very dissatisfied with my life & and altogether out of tune.

> 9 April 1885.   A day of incessant labour, but little to show. I cannot but think that there is something wrong with my brain ... I suppose I want a change but I cannot have it.

> 19 April 1885.   A day of intense & incessant labour, the result *one sentence*. I really think that there must be [something] wrong with my brain.

> 29 April 1885.   My temper today fearfully irritable & vicious.

> 25 May 1885.   I seem absolutely imbecile, as if my brain were soft pulp. What it will end in God knows.

> 28 May 1885.   Heard that I had not got the Merton Professorship. My depression & wretchedness was such that I couldn't settle to work in the evening. It would be impossible to

> conceive a state of more abject misery than I am in. The
> Oxford failure has however I feel sure nothing to do with
> it, since I was quite as bad before I knew.

14 July 1885.   Tonight I turned a corner. I did almost a quarter of
a page which will do very well.

2 October 1885.   As I have recorded the troubles let me record the
joy. This morning I carried the revised proofs of my
article on the Predecessors of Shakespeare to Mr Clowes
[printer of the *Quarterly*] . . . the article is finished & I have
already been complimented by Dr Smith and Murray.[5]

Though this was clearly the worst nightmare that Collins ever
went through when producing an article, they all caused him some
struggle and this was something which surfaced in his strong
irritation with any piece of writing which seemed to have been
produced without much effort.

Collins' review of Symonds' book, however, bore few signs of its
painful birth when it finally appeared in October 1885.[6] It was
lengthy, fifty-one pages, extremely forthright and magisterial,
with a hint of Jeffrey about it as well as Macaulay and with every
indication that it was intended to be a definitive statement on the
topic at hand. Symonds was no lightweight littérateur and Collins
began the review by drawing attention to his qualifications 'as an
accomplished and industrious man of letters'. His work on the
Greek poets, on Dante and on the Italian Renaissance was duly
noted and recommended and Collins conveyed the impression that
Symonds, if anyone, was exactly the right man to do justice to the
predecessors of Shakespeare topic. All of this of course was merely
a polite preamble (though Collins no doubt did genuinely respect
Symonds' learning in some fields): the book itself was a disappointing let-down; it was hurried, superficial, diffuse and repetitive. It
was a book to keep serious-minded students of English literature
well away from.

In his account of the book, Collins catalogued its faults much
more ruthlessly than earlier reviewers had. Instead of a carefully
researched study of the topic, 'What we found', said Collins, 'was,
we regret to say, every indication of precipitous haste, a style
which where it differs from the style of extemporary journalism
differs for the worse—florid, yet commonplace; full of impurities;

inordinately, nay, incredibly, diffuse and pleonastic; a narrative
clogged with endless repetitions, without symmetry, without proportion.' Remarks on Shakespeare and Marlowe, for example,
were endlessly repeated without significant variation and it
appeared that material previously published in journals had been
crudely incorporated into the book without proper revision and
adaptation. Allied to this—and Collins' fury with Symonds'
journalistic dash was clearly related to his own agonizing labours
in producing the review—there were several careless mistakes and
hints of skimming the subject: 'Has Mr Symonds never inspected
North's version of Guevara's *Relox de Principes*, George Pettie's
Petite Palace of Pettie, and Castiglione's *Il Cortegiano*?' If he had,
Collins grimly asserted, he would have known that Lyly, far from
inventing euphuism, was 'simply following a fashion'.[7]

In the normal way of things, one suspects that Collins might
have left it there and proceeded straight on to his own account of
pre-Shakespearean drama but on this occasion he had other
targets to aim at—namely Swinburne and the aesthetic movement. This—the first of many such attacks on the aesthetes and
aesthetic criticism—very clearly shows Collins deliberately dis-
tancing himself from Swinburne and any aesthetic influences he
may have come under during his Oxford days and declaring
himself the follower of Arnold and Carlyle. Symonds's book,
Collins argued, was a typical product of a movement bent on
reducing criticism to mere impression and personal caprice. The
leader of this pernicious movement was Swinburne (Pater is
implicated too) and under his influence a whole new generation of
aesthete-critics was busily undermining the whole foundation of
intelligent, objective criticism. The review of Symonds' book
therefore became the excuse for a savage attack on Swinburne the
critic. Much as Collins admired Swinburne the poet (surprisingly
in view of his growing dislike for the whole Swinburne school), he
found him a preposterous poseur when it came to criticism:

> Of the intellectual qualifications indispensable to a critic he has,
> with the exception of a powerful and accurate memory, literally
> none. His judgment is the sport sometimes of his emotions and
> sometimes of his imagination; and what is in men of normal temper
> the process of reflection, is in him the process of imagination
> operating on emotion, and of emotion reacting on imagination . . .

Criticism is with him neither a process of analysis nor a process of interpretation, but a 'lyrical cry'. Canons and principles, criteria and standards, he has none. His genius and temper as a critic are precisely those of Aristotle's young man. What seem to be Mr Swinburne's convictions are merely his temporary impressions. What he sees in one light in one mood, he sees in another light in another mood. He is, in truth, as inconsistent as he is intemperate, as dogmatic as he is whimsical—the very Zimri of criticism.[8]

Collins follows this brilliant sketch of Swinburne the demented critic by citing some of his 'ludicrous vagaries of opinion', his habit of veering in an instant from one extreme to another and his endless self-contradictions: 'The very qualities, for example, which attract him in Fletcher, repel him in Euripides. He overwhelms Byron with ribald abuse for precisely the same qualities which in Victor Hugo elicit from him fulsome eulogy.' Most of Swinburne's critical responses, said Collins, were nothing more than wild ranting outbursts: 'The very name of Marlowe appears to have the power of completely subjugating his reason.' And so on.

Through all this of course we can hear the endless, more or less convivial arguments about favourite writers which Collins and Swinburne engaged in around the dinner table or in walks over Putney Heath. Suddenly, however, Collins had publicly transposed things into a decidedly hostile key where Swinburne was shown to be so lacking in critical insight and consistency he was not worth listening to. After ten years of friendship Collins was plainly tired of deferring to Swinburne on critical questions and made the most of the Symonds review to publicize the fact. The surprising thing is that he waited so long before launching his all-out attack; Carlyle had told him years before that Swinburne and his school were a 'curious growth'[9] (and other critics of course since the mid-sixties had been saying the same thing), and regular meetings with Swinburne in the interim must have convinced Collins of his critical perversity. Swinburne of course offered him all kinds of valuable literary contacts and opened up doors that would have otherwise remained closed for him, but he must have often winced at Swinburne's pontifications and wild inconsistencies. In any case, by 1885, Collins felt sufficiently sure of himself to stand up to Swinburne publicly; Swinburne might be a poetic genius (Collins never questioned this for a moment) but his

pretensions to be taken for a serious literary critic needed explod-
ing. Collins also clearly felt the need to declare his own status as a
critic; he might be a failed poet, having written almost nothing
since his Oxford days, but as a critic he felt he had the credentials
to justify his putting Swinburne and Symonds in their place.

The extent to which Swinburne had directly influenced
Symonds of course remained an open question but Collins insisted
that the Swinburne influence was responsible for the florid, over-
emotional tone of much of Symonds' writing. Symonds for
example had spoken of a certain play as 'an asp, short, ash-
coloured, poison-fanged, blunt-headed, abrupt in movement, hiss-
ing and wriggling through the sands of human misery'; he
described a dramatist 'stabbing the metal plate on which he works,
drowning it in *aqua fortis* till it froths'; and spoke of 'the lust for the
impossible being injected like a molten fluid into all Marlowe's
eminent dramatic personalities'. And so on. This was the aesthete-
critic out-writing the authors he was supposed to be discussing;
simply using the work as a springboard for his own creative
impulses and urges. Collins himself of course was equally given to
forceful overstatement and rhetorical outbursts but not of this
overly Paterian kind, its self-conscious mannerisms advertising the
true aesthetic temperament. As a critic and moralist he felt
impelled to make a stand: 'the duty imposed on us as critics is, we
feel, imperative, and that duty would be ill performed if we did
not raise our voice against innovations which we believe to be
vicious and mischievous'.[10]

Having made his position clear, Collins then spent the rest of his
review—over forty pages—presenting his own view of the development of English drama before Shakespeare. As one would
expect, he presents a firm pedagogic account, along the lines of an
Extension lecture, showing how the thing should be done by a
clear-headed critic untouched by Swinburnian or Paterian
influence. Early English drama is methodically divided into three
epochs; Romantic drama is distinguished from older drama by
'three striking peculiarities'; the influence of Italian drama on
English is duly noted, and various other stages of development
accounted for before the arrival of the 'golden era' of Elizabethan
literature. At this stage Collins begins to assert his own judgments
and preferences. Marlowe, for example, is accorded significantly

less importance than Swinburne gave him, while Greene is given special prominence. Greene, for Collins, was a fascinating figure; a tragic case, torn between depravity and better feelings, suffering from religious hypochondria, struggling through a life of 'incessant literary activity' and always aware of his own follies and selfishness. Collins was always drawn to struggling genius of this kind and excuses the time he spends on Greene by saying: 'We have indulged ourselves in these remarks because we frankly own that Greene is a great favourite with us.'[11] This was certainly the case. Collins spent years researching Greene's life and works (he checked the registers of forty-two churches in Norwich to find the entry of Greene's baptism)[12] and in 1905 brought out an edition of his Plays and Poems.

Collins' systematic survey of sixteenth-century English drama, of course, was barely noticed by readers of his review—the main focus of attention was the attack on Swinburne and Symonds. Symonds was naturally deeply hurt by the review and, despite the consoling remarks of his friends, found his reputation as a scholar of Elizabethan drama badly damaged. Smith and Elder the publishers in fact discouraged him from writing a projected second volume on the subject.[13] Collins naturally protested that he had no personal quarrel with Symonds; he was merely performing his function as a responsible reviewer bound to tell the truth about the book in front of him. To underline this point, he reprinted the article in his *Essays and Studies* in 1895, after Symonds' death, arguing that 'Nothing could have justified the appearance of those strictures during Mr Symonds' lifetime if they are not equally justified when he lives only in the power and influence of his writings.'[14]

Collins always argued, and clearly genuinely believed, that he was a fairminded critic who attacked only the book not the author behind it and his belief in his own critical highmindedness was strengthened when Swinburne, far from showing any personal resentment at the treatment handed out to him, continued to write him friendly and often flattering letters—as he should have guessed, Swinburne had not yet come across the review; when he did Collins was quickly and savagely enlightened. This, however, was not until late the following year; in October 1885 Collins felt he had struck a decisive blow for serious critical standards and that his argument had been accepted by Swinburne if not by the deeply offended Symonds. Collins of course was unaware of the deeper currents of resentment and envy which underlay the firmly judicial and objective tone of the review; he resented the influence Swinburne exercised (or Collins supposed he exercised) as a critic and was affronted by Symonds' easy assumption of critical and scholarly expertise. He was also temperamentally out of sympathy with anything that smacked of aestheticism—with all that Carlylean earnestness in him—and refused to see anything but decadence in it: impressionistic criticism from this time on became an increasingly major target in his reviewing and he hunted it down not only in the work of presumed aesthetes like Richard Le Gallienne but also in that of academic critics like Gosse, Saintsbury and Raleigh. On the other hand, his case against the self-indulgent quest for fine excesses in critical writings had its point. If this was to be the normal state of literary criticism in England, then the more learned and supposedly disinterested critics—Collins among them—would find it hard to get a hearing. Moreover, if aestheticism spread unchecked there was much less chance of promoting serious literary studies—incorporated in schools of English—as Collins and like-minded people conceived of them. At one level, then, Collins' review settled certain personal scores against rivals and oppressive acquaintances; at another it more acceptably argued for critical discipline and scholarly rigour against impressionistic anarchy.

3

This mixture of motives was also evident in Collins' next article in the *Quarterly*—a review of Gosse's *From Shakespeare to Pope: An Inquiry into the Causes and Phenomena of the Rise of Classical Poetry in England* (1885). Gosse's book consisted of the Clark lectures he had given at Cambridge and was well-received when it appeared in May 1885. The *Athenaeum* reviewer, for example, called it a book to 'read twice and consult often', while the *Saturday Review* suavely likened it to 'good madeira wine from across the sea'.[15]

Collins meanwhile had been preoccupied with other matters and therefore did not get around to dealing with Gosse's book until the following year: first there was the review of Symonds' book to work on, then the publication of his own book on Bolingbroke and Voltaire. From early in 1886 he was also beginning to challenge the Oxford approach to English studies following Napier's arrival there. His first major articles on this issue appeared in the *Pall Mall Gazette* in May 1886 when he made his public debut as the champion of literary studies against philology. The philologists, said Collins, had already reduced the teaching of Classics to a barren discipline and now seemed likely to do the same for English literature. Napier's appointment to the Chair of English meant that there were now four chairs of philology in Oxford—Anglo-Saxon, Celtic, Comparative Philology and the Merton Chair, something which Collins found quite outrageous:

> That there should be no less than four chairs for the philological study of literature, that ample provision should be made for the interpretation of Caedmon and Beowulf, for the interpretation of the Gododin and the Tain Bo, for the interpretation of Robert of Gloucester and William Shoreham, but that the study of English literature as represented by the English classics should be absolutely unprovided for, is an anomaly so extraordinary, or, to speak plainly, so scandalous that it can scarcely fail to strike even university legislators.[16]

This was the article, it may be recalled, which Swinburne, still unaware of Collins' attack on him, lavishly praised in a letter to Collins in June 1886: 'I never read anything with more absolute sympathy or with more sincere gratitude . . .'[17] Collins' attack on philology was the prelude to an appeal for a new School of Literature where English literature would be studied alongside Classical literature:

> The study of the poetry, the oratory, the criticism, of Greece and Rome pursued side by side with that of our own would at once place the study of the classics on the only footing on which in modern times it is possible to justify it, and at the same time raise the study of English literature to its proper level in education.[18]

The review of Gosse's book in the October 1886 number of the *Quarterly*[19] served as a follow up to this appeal. It also served to highlight both Gosse's incompetence as a literary historian and the scandal of log-rolling by which second-rate books were hailed as literary masterpieces. *From Shakespeare to Pope*, etc., published by the University Press and puffed by friendly reviews turned out to be an affront to the idea of literary history; it was carelessly written, packed with errors of fact, and full of misleading judgments. Collins' opening statement showed him to be in a mood for pronouncing extreme penalties: 'That such a book as this should have been permitted to go forth to the world with the *imprimatur* of the University of Cambridge, affords matter for very grave reflection.' Gosse's book— much more even than Symonds'—was a sign of corrupt times, when worthless books were palmed off on to a gullible public by 'literary charlatans' who would stop at nothing 'for the sake of exalting themselves into a factitious reputation'. 'Indeed', said Collins, with a touch of Gissing-like bitterness,

> things have come to such a pass, that persons of real merit, if they have the misfortune to depend on their pens for a livelihood, must either submit to be elbowed and jostled out of the field, or take part in the same ignoble scramble for notoriety, and the same detestable system of mutual puffery.[20]

Within the first three or four pages the high-pitched note of personal anger was struck—Gosse was no longer the former friend and ally, whose literary work gave Collins so much pleasure; he was now the chief offender in a system of corruption and fraud. As always happened with Collins' major quarrels, the old friend now represented something hostile to his most important interests—his uncle represented the ugly world of commerce, Swinburne the Art for Art's sake movement, Gosse the literary cliques who dominated the publishing world and kept out 'persons of real merit'.

Despite the quirky onesidedness of all this, Collins had a strong case to argue once he got down to examining Gosse's book. Gosse may have been a versatile critic but he showed himself to be amazingly casual and lax in *From Shakespeare to Pope*. Collins as an expert in matters of facts and dates was able to detail a staggering list of elementary blunders in the book and to hold the Clark Lecturer up to ridicule. Gosse, for example, had apparently not known whether Sidney's *Arcadia* and Harrington's *Oceana* were in prose or verse; he had confused the two Harringtons of the period, and the first Earl of Shaftesbury with the third; he had claimed that between 1660 and 1760 Milton and Roscommon were the only poets writing in blank verse (Collins cited at least twenty-six others who were), and so on through page after page of the book.[21] Gosse had been equally slapdash when it came to dates: 'Indeed, Mr Gosse appears to be incapable of transcribing a date correctly, even when it must have been before his very eyes.' Examples were provided of this. Gosse's easy-going narrative also cut right through basic matters of fact turning literary history into literary fiction at several points. Collins cannot resist from quoting one of these passages at length:

> the following is so exquisitely characteristic, not only of Mr Gosse himself but of the Dilettanti School generally, that we cannot pass it by. 'Late in the summer, one handsome and gallant young fellow'—Mr Gosse is speaking of the death of Sidney Godolphin— 'riding down the deep-leaved lanes that led from Dartmoor . . . met a party of Roundheads, was cut down and killed' (p. 109). Now Sidney Godolphin was killed at the end of January 1642/3, when the lanes were, we apprehend, not deep-leaved; he was, it may be added, not handsome, for Clarendon especially enlarges on the meanness of his person; he was not 'cut down and killed', he was shot dead by a musket ball; he was not meeting a party of Roundheads in the lanes, he was pursuing them into Chagford.[22]

Gosse had plainly neglected Mark Pattison's advice to spend several years reading up a subject before setting pen to paper.[23]

Gosse's abilities as a literary historian were one thing, but this was the man appointed by Cambridge University as Clark Lecturer and whose lectures had been acclaimed by the literary world. Collins' exposure of the book's nonsensical claims to be a serious 'Inquiry into the Causes and Phenomena of the Rise of Classical Poetry in England' (as the subtitle had it) conveniently prepared the way for another of his appeals for a proper School of Literature where such aberrations would be impossible:

> Of the necessity of the Universities directing their attention to this important subject, no further proof is required than the contrast between the high standard of classical, historical, and scientific teaching throughout the kingdom and the deplorably low standard, all but universal, in the teaching of English literature . . . A work analogous to the work which stands at the head of this article would, we believe, in any other department of learning and culture,

be impossible. One tithe of its blunders and absurdities would have ruined instantly a book treating of Greek or Roman poetry, or discussing some point in modern history.[24]

Gosse's book like Symonds' therefore provided Collins with ready material to deal with larger objectives—the Art for Art's sake movement, the literary cliques, and the universities' disregard of literature.

Not surprisingly again the main argument of the review was completely lost sight of—the sensational attack on Gosse got the most attention. Reviews in the *Quarterly* were published anonymously but it was soon discovered that Collins was the author and a tremendous uproar broke out in the literary world—for several weeks the journals were full of it. Gosse himself was devastated by it; he had never received such a mauling before: 'the *Quarterly review*', he wrote to Thomas Hardy, 'has felled, flayed, eviscerated, pulverized and blown to the winds poor Me in thirty pages of good round abuse . . . It is rather shocking, and keeps me awake o'nights and affects my liver. But I hope to live it down.'[25] Tennyson comforted him with his 'louse on the locks of literature' comment on Collins, but it took him a long time to recover his equilibrium and made him a more cautious literary historian in the future. He published a lengthy reply to Collins in the *Athenaeum* on 23 October 1886, but even his best friends thought it hopelessly inadequate— Symonds for example called it 'ridiculously feeble'.[26]

Collins, however, came out of it much worse. In the journals he was marked out as brutal and vindictive; the *Pall Mall Gazette*, for example, declared 'never since Macaulay annihilated Croker in the *Edinburgh* do we remember to have seen so cruel a castigation as that which Macaulay's disciple now administers in the *Quarterly* to Mr Edmund Gosse'.[27] Everyone knew that Collins had earlier been on good terms with Gosse and was now repaying Gosse's kindly attentions with contempt and abuse. Worse still, Collins clearly relished his attack. William Archer, one of Gosse's friends, wrote: 'When a man who has broken bread with you . . . finds himself impelled by a stern sense of duty to tear you limb from limb he should in decency make some attempt to conceal the exultation with which he goes about that friendly office.'[28] Trinity College Cambridge affirmed its support of Gosse, and contempt for Collins, by re-electing Gosse to the Clark Lectureship for a further term and there were clear indications that the literary establishment was closing ranks against Collins the pugnacious outsider. Since the review had attacked the literary world and the universities, as well as Gosse himself, it was not difficult to feel that Collins was everyone's enemy.

Collins, however, ably defended himself and answered Gosse's pathetic reply by a detailed examination of his arguments. Gosse's defence of some of his mistakes was easily demolished—like other of Collins' opponents he was no match for him in the area of scholarly argument. Collins could confidently assert, very much in the tone of his schoolboy arrogance twenty years earlier,[29] that 'it will be seen that in every case where Mr Gosse has accused me of misinterpreting his words, I have done no such thing, and that in every case he has asserted that I was wrong and he right, he is in the wrong and I am in the right'.[30] As for Gosse's charge that he had acted maliciously, Collins found it 'preposterous',

> and Mr Gosse must know that it is preposterous. It is quite true that I was some eight years ago on friendly terms with him; it is quite true that I was his guest and that he has been my guest. In those days I believed him to be an honest student and an honest worker, and at that time, some six or more years ago, I never grudged my cordial testimony to the abilities which, in the volume I have reviewed, he has so sadly abused ... Since then we became gradually estranged, in the sense, at least, that we seldom or never met—for the last five or six years, if my memory serves me rightly, we have not exchanged a word—but we never quarrelled. He went his way, I went mine.[31]

Collins went on to insist that he had no reason to bear Gosse any grudge—particularly since Gosse had paid him a 'high compliment' on p. 30 of the book—and had never had any ambition to be Clark Lecturer himself.

So far so good, but then Collins made a fatal mistake. In order to point out to Gosse that it was possible to accept criticism without feeling personally insulted, he referred to his attack on Swinburne the previous year:

> having last year to review in the *Quarterly* Mr Symonds's 'Shakspere's predecessors in the English Drama'—a work which illus-

trated the mischievous influence of Mr Swinburne's criticism and style—I wrote as severe an attack on Mr Swinburne as a critic and prose writer as I could possibly devise. But I have yet to learn that Mr Swinburne considers me 'no gentleman', or complains of 'mortal wounds given by an estranged' etc. On the contrary, the last communication I had from him was a generous eulogy of some trifle I had recently written, and hearty wishes of success.[32]

Swinburne of course had known nothing of all this until Collins mentioned it and instantly put an end to his naive notions of tolerance and generosity. A week later the *Athenaeum* was humming with Swinburne's abusive remarks on the *Quarterly* and its upstart reviewer. Swinburne, who a few months earlier had flattered Collins by comparing him with Macaulay, now called him Macaulay's 'ape', quibbled with his language, derided his opinions, and said he was glad to hear that he had been attacked by this reviewer: 'May the God of letters preserve me from the deep disgrace of ever deserving his commendation!'[33] A week later Collins made a rueful reply, refuted particular points that Swinburne had raised, and offered him some advice: 'I would suggest to Mr Swinburne that he will best consult his reputation by avoiding controversy unless he can contrive to provide himself with better weapons than mere ribald abuse, deliberate misstatement, deliberberate misrepresentation, and sheer nonsense.'[34] After this, of course, the old friendly, even intimate, relationship between the two men came to an abrupt end. Collins, who retained his admiration for Swinburne the poet, was deeply hurt by the quarrel and in his naive way felt he had done nothing to personally offend Swinburne. Through Theodore Watts-Dunton, Swinburne's close friend and guardian, he made several attempts to patch things up without success. Eventually a meeting was arranged in February 1900, but predictably the evening was a disaster; Collins was contrite but Swinburne was distant and formal.[35] They never met again.

The Collins-Gosse-Swinburne storm rumbled on for a week or so, and most observers seemed to feel that Collins had overstepped the line of fair reviewing. Old friendships apart, he had not merely attacked Gosse and Swinburne, he had set out to destroy their reputations and publicly humiliate them as individuals. He had also used both the Symonds and the Gosse reviews as propagandist weapons in his larger campaign against the literary and educational worlds, and both men could justifiably feel they had been set up in an underhand way. Collins from this time on was treated warily by literary men, though his reviews—provocative and controversial as they were—were always welcomed by editors with an eye for a crackling dispute. Gosse, like Swinburne, never forgave Collins the blow to his reputation and years later was still referring bitterly to 'Shirt 'n Collars'.[36] In the Gosse and Swinburne circles after 1886 Collins was a name to conjure up all the worst feelings.

Yet, as objective onlookers had to admit, Collins was absolutely right in what he said about *From Shakespeare to Pope*. The book *was* a disgrace to literary scholarship, and while it continued in print for some time, no one took it seriously. Even Trinity College Cambridge, which re-elected Gosse to the Clark Lectureship out of sheer defiance had to admit the book was an 'aberration', and soon other contributors to the journals were finding fault with Gosse's scholarship in other areas—for example in his edition of Gray's poems.[37] News of the affair soon reached the United States, and an American correspondent claimed that no one who had heard Gosse lecture there was at all surprised at Collins' review—sophomores at American universities knew far more about seventeenth and eighteenth century literature than Gosse.[38] Jokes about Gosse circulated for months at Oxford—in the *Oxford Magazine* for example he appeared as Mr Plucked Gosseling weaving 'a network of gracious sentences', surrounding 'the images of departed genius with fragrant epithet', and delighting 'the ear of a confiding public with cloudy criticism and dubious summary'.[39] What nobody pointed out was the fact that, until Collins' review, *From Shakespeare to Pope* was accepted as a work of sound scholarship and persuasive criticism. Collins might have been shaken by his quarrel with Swinburne, but he could take some comfort from other reactions to his review.

NOTES

1   *The Life and Letters of Sir Edmund Gosse*, ed. Evan Charteris, 1931, p. 197.

2   For Symonds' life and career, see Phyllis Grosskurth, *John Addington Symonds*, 1964.

3   Ibid., p. 228.

4   L. C. Collins, op. cit., p. 234.

5   Notebooks, Birmingham University Library.

6   J. C. Collins, 'Shakspere's Predecessors in the English Drama', *Quarterly Review*, CLXI, October 1885, pp. 330–81.

7   Ibid., pp. 330–33.

8   Ibid., 335–36.

9   L. C. Collins, op. cit., p. 44.

10 'Shakspere's Predecessors in the English Drama', p. 337–38.

11 Ibid., p. 370.

12 L. C. Collins, op. cit., p. 232n.

13 Phyllis Grosskurth, op. cit.,p. 229.

14 J. C. Collins, *Essays and Studies*, p. viii.

15 See the *Pall Mall Gazette*, 30 October 1886, p. 1.

16 *Pall Mall Gazette*, 31 May 1886, p. 11.

17 See above, p. 25.

18 *Pall Mall Gazette*, 31 May 1886, p. 12.

19 J. C. Collins, 'English Literature at the Universities', *Quarterly Review*,CLXIII, October 1886, pp. 289–329.

20 Ibid., p. 293.

21 Ibid., pp. 295–96.

22 Ibid., p. 300.

23 See above, p. 28.

24 'English Literature at the Universities', p. 328.

25 *The Life and Letters of Sir Edmund Gosse*, p. 201.

26 Phyllis Grosskurth, op. cit., p. 230.

27 *Pall Mall Gazette*, 15 October 1886, p. 11.

28 Ibid., 23 October 1886, p. 9.

29 See above, p. 6.

30 *Athenaeum*, 30 October 1886, p. 568.

31 Ibid., p. 569.

32 Ibid., p. 569.

33 Ibid., 6 November 1886, p. 600.

34 Ibid., 13 November 1886, p. 636.

35 L. C. Collins, op. cit., pp. 153–54. Theodore Watts-Dunton, Swinburne's legal adviser, literary confidant and from 1879 onwards virtual protector, acted as a reluctant go-between for Collins and Swinburne. Watts-Dunton never forgave Collins for attacking Swinburne but nonetheless remained in contact with him. The five surviving letters from Collins to Watts-Dunton show Collins assi-

duously cultivating his acquaintance, praising his poems, inviting him to meet figures like Stephen Phillips, and generally being deferential to his opinions. These letters are in the Brotherton Library, University of Leeds.

36 *The Life and Letters of Sir Edmund Gosse*, p. 279.

37 *Pall Mall Gazette*, 17 November 1886, pp. 11–12.

38 Ibid., 21 October 1886, p. 6.

39 *Oxford Magazine*, 4 May 1887, p. 175. Collins later reviewed Gosse's *A Short History of Modern English Literature* (1898) and repeated his charges about Gosse's carelessness and inaccuracy. Here, however, he was more objective in his summing up of Gosse's abilities as a critic: Gosse had a wide knowledge of Belles Lettres from the seventeenth to the nineteenth century and though far from being a 'sound' critic was a 'sympathetic' one; 'he has an agreeable but somewhat affected style, and can gossip pleasantly and plausibly about subjects which are within the range indicated'. Outside this range he was at the mercy of his handbooks. J. C. Collins, *Ephemera Critica*, 1901, pp. 111 ff. Collins' assessment of Gosse as a versatile but trivial critic came to be accepted as a fair one from 1886 onwards, though Gosse continued to exercise considerable influence as a man of letters and log-roller.

CHAPTER FIVE

THE OXFORD DISPUTE

Collins' involvement in the English studies dispute at Oxford from 1886 onwards has been touched on by Stephen Potter in *The Muse in Chains* (1937) and by D. J. Palmer in *The Rise of English Studies* (1965). In the first Collins appears as a central though absurdly arrogant and overbearing figure, and in the second as a more peripheral one; an earnest interferer but someone not fully aware of the main issues. Neither assessment does proper justice to his contribution to the debate. Collins certainly hectored and wrangled, pushed and cajoled but between 1886 and 1894, when the Oxford English school was set up, he also presented a case for literary studies which, with some modifications, came to be accepted as the most convincing one.

The Merton appointment in 1885 brought the argument about the nature of English studies to the fore, but the opposition between the philologists and the literary men was apparent when the question of an English Chair was discussed before the University Commission in 1877. To some English was properly a matter of language studies and ought to be closely allied to the study of Anglo-Saxon and Comparative Philology already established at Oxford; for others English meant chiefly 'English literature' which ought to be connected either with History or Classics.[1] The argument which later broke out at the time of the Merton election, showed the state of confusion which reigned where English was concerned. The fact that the Chair was given to a philologist, however, underlined the fact that English literature as such was seen by many at Oxford as a lightweight dilettante subject, not substantial enough for serious academic study.

In many ways the philologists could put forward the most convincing arguments at this time. Philology was an exacting study which had rapidly gained prestige in the academic world during the nineteenth century, particularly in Germany, but also in English universities. English literature on the other hand, while it might figure in some examination syllabuses, was essentially a popular subject, easy to get up, lacking in rigour and clearly inferior to other subjects as an academic discipline. As the *Oxford Magazine* put it in October 1886: 'Now English literature, as a subject of examination, has had its trial . . . It was found to be, of all subjects, the most convenient to the crammer, the most useless as a test of ability or of knowledge.'[2] Examinations apart, there were other reasons for promoting the interests of philology over those of English literature in the universities: there was a danger of a takeover by European scholars where the advanced study of English philology was concerned. Important work had been started on the editing of early English texts, on dialects, and on the compilation of a new English dictionary, but much remained to be done. Walter Skeat put the problem squarely in 1891:

> Perhaps there is no greater subject of reproach to the English Nation at large, than the fact that the true value of our magnificent language should have been left in a great measure for foreigners to discover. If we enquire who was the first person to write an Anglo-Saxon grammar of any scientific value, we find that the answer leads us to Erasmus Rask, a Dane. If we ask where such a thing as a really scientific grammar of the English language, planned on a sufficient and adequate scale, is to be found, the answer is, that there are three such works of considerable importance—one by Koch, one by Mätzner, and one by Fiedler and Sachs: they are all written in German, by German authors. If we ask for a scientific treatise on the subject of English metre, we are referred to one written in German, by Dr. Schipper of Vienna.[3]

The drive to set up chairs of philology and schools of philology was clearly related to this sense of English backwardness, and, at Oxford, with chairs of Comparative Philology, Anglo-Saxon, Celtic, and English there was a strong language lobby in the University and any projected School of English would be sure to reflect its interests.

2

By early 1886, in fact, it was apparent that Oxford was planning a new School of Modern Languages along the lines of the recently set up Medieval and Modern Languages Tripos at Cambridge. English was one of the studies offered at Cambridge but the chief emphasis was on language and early literature.[4] Ideas about the new school at Oxford were aired in the *Academy* during January, February and March 1886. One suggestion by Sweet involved the study of the English language in all its phases; English literature in all its periods; the Germanic languages; Old French and the Romance languages; and the Celtic languages.[5] A week later Sweet urged Oxford to follow Cambridge as quickly as possible: 'Now is the time to found a School of Modern Philology. In a few years it may be too late. The Germans will have annexed the subject.'[6] Despite the inclusion of English literature in Sweet's scheme, and the suspicion was that this was merely a sop to the opposition, the literary men strongly objected to the whole scheme. The cause of modern English literature was defended by Sidney Lee, then assistant editor of the *Dictionary of National Biography*, who argued that literature was allied to history rather than philology, that 'English literature of the last two hundred years is not the least important part of the subject', and that the subject should not be dragged into the Oxford curriculum 'at the skirts of Germanic philology'.[7] Such defences of modern literature were made at regular intervals from this point on.[8]

Collins meanwhile was preparing his own contributions to the general debate. His articles in the *Pall Mall Gazette* in May 1886 have already been referred to and his review of Gosse's book, making yet another appeal for a School of Literature, followed in October. By this time he had also been writing round to distinguished people for support in a public campaign both to oppose the projected School of Modern Languages and to promote his own scheme. A new School of Literature, where English and Classical literature came together, would be desirable in itself, would give Classical studies a much needed boost, would be a training ground for teachers of English literature in the Extension Movement and elsewhere, and would become a centre for serious—as opposed to dilettante—literary research; just the kind of school in fact that Collins would himself like to head.

His campaign was mainly conducted—with the co-operation of the editor W. T. Stead—in the columns of the *Pall Mall Gazette*, though it soon spilled over into other papers and journals when Gosse and Swinburne were drawn into it. The first letter appeared on 22 October 1886 when T. H. Huxley, in answer to Collins's call, provocatively called the establishment of chairs of philology under the name of literature 'a fraud practised on letters'.[9] This was immediately refuted by Max Müller, Professor of Comparative Philology at Oxford, who defended Napier's appointment and divulged the fact that plans were going ahead for a 'School of Modern Literature' (sic!), similar to the one suggested by Sweet, consisting of Teutonic, Romanic and Celtic studies where English literature would take its bearings from Teutonic rather than classical sources.[10]

These opening contributions were followed by a series of replies to a questionnaire which Collins had circulated to a number of influential men. The questionnaire posed three questions:

1. Was it desirable that the universities should provide systematic instruction in English literature?

2. Was it desirable that a distinction should be made between Philology and Literature, and that the instruction provided should be instruction in Literature as distinguished from instruction in Philology?

3. Was it desirable that the study of English Literature should be indissolubly associated with the study of ancient Classical Literature?

Among those who provided replies to the questions were included certain Heads of Oxford colleges, leading politicians like Gladstone and Bright, famous literary figures like Matthew Arnold, Tennyson and William Morris (but not Swinburne!), literary critics like Pater and Symonds (but not Gosse!), representatives of the Church and the Law, and a miscellaneous group of Professors, Headmasters and examiners in English literature. Such was the response and the interest aroused that at the end of January 1887 a special reprint of the replies was issued because it was 'no longer possible to meet the demand for copies of the papers containing this or that eminent man's opinion'. The same month, to give even further publicity to the campaign, Collins included a substantial number of the extracts in an article he wrote for the *Quarterly*.

Most of those who sent in replies were strongly in favour of English literature as a university subject, though serious doubts were expressed by William Morris,[11] Walter Pater,[12] and Grant Allen[13] (Allen, who was at King Edward's Birmingham with Collins, was not formally approached for his view but sent it in anyway). These doubts could more or less be summed up in Allen's comment: 'If you wish to kill a study, make it the subject of academical teaching.' Others, including Matthew Arnold and W. J. Courthope,[14] thought that it would be better to add some English texts to existing classical syllabuses at Oxford rather than set up a new School of Literature as Collins was suggesting. This was a view probably shared by most Oxford classicists, partly out of a general dislike of radical innovation, partly out of a fear that a new School of Literature would put Classics in a subordinate position to English literature. But apart from a handful of objections to the whole idea of making English literature an academic subject, and the doubts about the right way to fit it into the Oxford curriculum, the replies indicated a large measure of support for the study of English literature and especially for the study of literature as opposed to philology.

At this stage, Collins was getting some encouragement from Oxford itself, and especially from Jowett. Jowett, who seems to have been rather taken aback by Collins' sudden leap into polemics, wrote to him on 21 October 1886 asking whether he was the acting editor of the *Pall Mall Gazette*.[15] Jowett had been asked for an opinion about the article on Gosse by the editor, who in fact was acting on Collins' instructions. Jowett was not prepared to become involved in the Collins–Gosse wrangle, but he was willing to support the cause of English literature provided of course that classical interests were safeguarded and agreed that the best thing would be for Collins to follow up the questionnaire exercise with an article in the *Quarterly Review*:

> Your article might touch (1) on the importance to the study of Classical Literature of its association with modern because that gives new interest to it. It is getting in some respects worn out, and that would breathe a new life into it. (2) On the necessity of the knowledge of the classics for the intelligent study of modern literature—far greater clearly than for the study of the early stages of English literature, even of Chaucer, with that view.[16]

Jowett, however, like other Oxford classicists, was wary about Collins' proposal for a whole new School of Literature. In his January article in the *Quarterly Review*, Collins followed Jowett's advice fairly closely but repeated his call for a new School of Literature. As a sop to those who feared that a new school would draw students away from Greats, he suggested that the latter might be made a compulsory preliminary to his School of Literature.[17]

Collins' polemics, however, caused extreme affront in some Oxford quarters. He might be a Balliol man but he had no cause to be meddling in internal Oxford affairs. The *Oxford Magazine*, always jealous of Oxford's rights and privileges, took a dim view of his public campaign in support of his opinions: 'Mr Churton Collins, having demolished Mr Gosse, has now returned to his alternative occupation, dogmatic dictation to the Universities.' Collins claimed to speak for 'the whole nation' on the issue, but 'when we come to enquire as to how this national voice has expressed itself, we find that it is in the form either of private letters to Mr Collins, or of contributions to the *Pall Mall Gazette*.'[18] A few months later Collins was parodied by the magazine as Mr Random Tearem who appeared in a satirical playlet along with Mr Sentimental Screamer (W. T. Stead, editor of the *Pall Mall Gazette*);[19] a burlesque Collins declaims: 'I have rescued literature from the slough into which Pedantry, Dilettantism, and Sciolism have conspired to sink it. The eyes of civilised Europe are fixed upon me ...' etc.[20] Collins' truculence, fervour and assertiveness always left him open to either mere dislike or puerile jokes.

Despite the campaign, the letters and the articles, the plans for a School of Modern Languages—as opposed to Literature—made steady headway in the spring of 1887. English was one of the subjects proposed, but not of course in the form the literary men wanted. This being so, Collins tried to use his Extension connexions in an effort to block the progress of the proposed school. In April, the Right Hon. George Goschen, President of the London Society for the Extension of University Teaching (and one of Collins' referees for the Merton Chair), was persuaded to write to the Vice-Chancellor of Oxford about the whole scheme. Goschen pointed out that English literature was the most popular subject in the Extension courses, but that there was a shortage of really good teachers in it. This he said was due 'to the want of any regular training in the subject' and he urged the University to put English literature on a proper footing in its Honours curriculum.[21] In June Collins followed this up with an appeal to the Oxford University Extension Committee, asking if he could meet them to discuss possible action in support of his campaign. The committee, however, were reluctant to get involved in a row with their superiors and declined his request, saying that the general view was that the School of Modern Languages would provide a good training for Extension lecturers.[22] Collins tried a similar appeal to the London Society without success. 'Very cheering after all my efforts & toil!', he wrote in his notebook, 'Such is the reward. However we have not said die yet! It is heartbreaking work.'[23]

Heartbreaking work certainly, yet Collins' campaign was helping to clarify particular issues and arguments in the University. In Congregation on 3 May, for example, the Provost of Oriel, D. B. Monro, referred to the articles in the *Pall Mall Gazette* as important factors in the discussion. Similarly, the Warden of Wadham, G. E. Thorley, pointed out that 'if the statute was in response to a demand from without, that demand was for a School of Literature, and the statute offered a School of Philology'.[24] If nothing else, Collins had helped to polarize the debate with considerable effect: there was a national demand for a School of Literature, as evidenced by the opinions Collins had managed to get together, while Oxford—or at least an influential part of it—persisted in setting up a narrow, specialist school which no one but budding philologists would have the slightest interest in. As Collins realized, whatever the doubts about the precise details of his own proposals, his main arguments on behalf of literary studies would appeal to all those at Oxford who disliked the look of the new philological school. By presenting these arguments in the name of the larger world of literature and education, or even of the 'nation' itself, he was thus able to bring the philologists under a certain amount of pressure with the aid of his Oxford allies. After further debates at Oxford, in fact, the proposal of the new school was finally defeated in Congregation on 1 November 1887. No one could reasonably doubt that Collins' campaign had played a significant part in this defeat.

3

By November 1887, then, a year after the Gosse review and the *Pall Mall Gazette* campaign, Collins was seen variously as a celebrated and notorious figure in the literary and educational worlds. He was the respected spokesman for the Extension Movement on literary questions, a 'louse on the locks of literature' for Gosse and his friends, and an ignorant troublemaker for certain factions at Oxford. For these last groups, particularly the philologists, he was seen as a mere literary amateur, intent on setting up a pleasant pursuit for undergraduates and Extension students. In a reply to a letter Collins wrote to the *Times* on behalf of his scheme on 1 June 1887, the Professor of Anglo-Saxon at Oxford, John Earle, wrote: 'The region of *belles lettres* is one that is very pleasant to ramble in, but one that is exceedingly difficult to reduce to a definite and teach-worthy system.'[25] This of course was a travesty of Collins' real position, but it formed the basis of the philologist's professional objections to his ideas and reappeared in what became the best-known, or even definitive, refutation of the literary approach—E. A. Freeman's article 'Literature and Language' in the October 1887 number of the *Contemporary Review*.

Freeman, who was Regius Professor of Modern History, at Oxford, was a member of the committee which had appointed Napier to the Merton Chair. Naturally he strongly resented the attack on Napier and on the whole philological approach to English and in May 1887 in a debate in Congregation had described the literary approach as 'mere chatter about Shelley'.[26] Now, in his October article, he recounted how he had acted in good faith in recommending Napier and was later amazed to find that there was a movement to set up a school of English 'which did not require a knowledge of the earliest forms of the English language, or a comparison of those forms with those of kindred languages'. There had even been talk of a 'fraud on literature' and an endless flow of letters and articles attacking the proposed School of Modern Languages in the name of literature and the Extension Movement.[27]

Freeman then came to the crux of his argument—that is, that not every pleasing and interesting subject was suitable for academic study:

> there are many studies which nobody wishes to disparage, studies
> which some men do well to pursue and which they may very well
> make the work of their lives, but which may still be quite unsuited
> to be subjects for the B.A. examination . . . We do not want, we will
> not say frivolous subjects, but subjects which are merely light,
> elegant, interesting. As subjects for examination we must have
> subjects in which it is possible to examine.[28]

If English literature by itself became an examination subject for
the Honours degree, since it was not possible to teach 'appreciation', some substitute would be taught instead; namely literary
facts and mere gossip about literature. Freeman's article received
much publicity at the time for its airy dismissal of literary studies
and was answered in more than one place.[29] Collins was not
mentioned by name, but it is obvious from the references to the
attack on the universities, to the literary applicants for the Merton
Chair, and to the subsequent campaign for literature, that Freeman had him in mind as the chief exponent of the 'light literary'
point of view. Again it completely misrepresented his idea of the
serious study of literature and made no mention of his case for
associating English with Classics. It was precisely because English
literary studies were in danger of falling to the level of dilettante
ramblings—witness Gosse's Clark Lectures—that Collins wanted
them set up on a firm academic basis.

As it happened, Collins had already prepared an answer to the
question 'Can English literature be taught?' when Freeman's
article appeared. As so often, Collins' article only appeared after
painful labour:

> Have just posted, Sep. 13th 1887, to Knowles for the *Nineteenth
> Century* an article on Can English Literature be Taught? it cost me
> *three weeks' work* at Oxford—very hard and intense work, but I am
> thoroughly dissatisfied with it & shouldn't be at all surprised if
> Knowles rejects it. I hate these abstract subjects. I remember the
> waking depression & those miserable walks round the Park before
> breakfast—three times I nearly abandoned it, hopeless of treating
> the subject properly. Done at last very well, published in Nov.
> number, 1887.[30]

Again, Collins' forthright and overbearing manner can be seen to
cover a sense of futility and self-doubt and each complete article
represented a triumph of determination and persistence. In the

present instance, as in most others, the finished result was compre-
hensive and convincing, given current critical assumptions,
though, as usual, allowance had to be made for Collins' utopian
visions.

Collins began by admitting that English literature was often a
failure in modern education:

> Teachers perceive with perplexity that it attains none of the ends
> which a subject in itself so full of attraction and interest might be
> expected to attain. It fails, they complain, to fertilise; it fails to
> inform; it fails even to awaken curiosity.[31]

This was because it had been approached in the wrong ways:

> It has been regarded not as the expression of art and genius, but as
> mere material for the study of words, as mere pabulum for
> philology. All that constitutes its intrinsic value has been ignored.
> All that constitutes its value as a liberal study has been ignored. Its
> masterpieces have been resolved into exercises in grammar, syntax,
> and etymology. Its history has been resolved into a barren cata-
> logue of names, works, and dates. No faculty but the faculty of
> memory has been called into play in studying it. That it should
> therefore have failed as an instrument of education is no more than
> might have been expected. But it has failed for the same reason that
> 'classics' have failed. It has failed not because it affords no material
> for profitable teaching, but because we pervert it into material for
> unprofitable teaching.[32]

Where appreciation of literature was attempted in the classroom,
too often it consisted of 'vague and florid declamations in the
aesthetic style'; evidence of Swinburne's all-pervasive and pernicious influence.

What was urgently needed where English literature was concerned was a proper clarification of aims together with the setting
up of the subject on a liberal basis at Oxford and Cambridge.
Collins denied that English literature could not be profitably
taught because it was liable to cramming on the side of literary
history and dissolved into mere impressionism on the side of
criticism. True, English literature was often crammed but then so
was History (Freeman's subject) and other subjects too. It was
certainly possible to set thought-provoking questions on literary
history and, equally, critical questions could be set requiring

knowledge and intelligence to answer; questions directed to matters of form and style, ethics and thought. The properly trained teacher of English literature would not simply indulge in impressionistic effusions on particular works, but would concern himself with basic critical issues—the issues of description, definition, analysis and evaluation.

Collins concluded with a paraphrase of Arnold's moral defence of literature, assigning to the teacher a task far above Freeman's notion of the aesthetic idler. The teacher, said Collins,

> will teach us to see in all poetry, not purely lyrical or simply fanciful, a criticism of life, sound or unsound, adequate or defective. And if in dealing with such luminaries as Chaucer and Spenser, as Shakespeare, Milton and Wordsworth, his care will not extend beyond reverent exposition, in dealing with the lesser lights, with our Drydens and our Popes, with our Byrons and our Shelleys, he will have another task. He will have to show how, in various degrees, defects of temper, the accidents of life, historical and social environment, and the like have obscured and distorted that vision which penetrates through the local and particular to the essential and universal.[33]

This by way of Arnold, Taine and Carlyle was Collins at his most rhapsodic and morally impassioned, though how this kind of 'reverent exposition' of great luminaries squared with the academic and the critical study of literature is far from clear. However, behind the grand manner of all this, lay a simple belief: if Homer and Virgil could be taught as great teachers of mankind, why not Shakespeare and Milton? Collins was pleased enough with his article to reprint it, along with others, in *The Study of English Literature* (1891), which if not actually the first book of its kind in England, was certainly the most provocative and emphatic.

Collins had made a good general case for taking English literature as seriously as any other subject in the curriculum; the main problem was that he was forced by the very nature of the dispute into extreme positions: the more his opponents underrated the substance and value of English literature as an academic subject, the more Collins felt the need to stress its potential scope and weight. The result was that by the time his book *The Study of English Literature* appeared, his School of Literature was beginning to look grossly overweight. He reminded his readers that he was pleading a 'counsel of perfection' but all the same his scheme was offered as a possibility, harking back in its scope to the pre-1850 School of Literae Humaniores at Oxford which involved 'Science' (Ethics, Rhetoric and Criticism), 'History', and 'Poetry'.

In its final form, in 1891, Collins's School consisted of four main groups of study: Poetry, Rhetoric, Criticism, and Miscellaneous prose literature. The main principle of the School was comparative study, and in each group the set works were taken from classical and modern literatures. Thus in the poetry section, selections from Homer, Sophocles, Virgil and Horace would be studied in close connexion with selections from Chaucer, Spenser, Shakespeare and Pope. The same pattern was followed in the other sections. The examinations would test the candidates' sense of the general evolution of literature as well as their knowledge of particular works. There were to be six papers in all, together with a thesis question, covering the fields of English History, the History of English literature, comparative literature (i.e. English literature in relation to classical, Italian and French literature), and literary criticism. In offering sample examination questions, Collins set out to go beyond the ordinary run-of-the-mill examination questions of the day, opting for thesis-length topics:

Describe the world of Chaucer on its social, political, and ecclesiastical sides. Account historically for Chaucer's attitude towards religion and politics.

Trace to their origin the following metres—blank verse, ottava rima, terza rima, the rhyme royal, the Spenserian stanza, the canzone, the sestine, enumerating the chief poems written in each, and pointing out with illustrative reference any modifications which these metres may have undergone in the hands of eminent English poets.

In what way, and to what extent has 'Platonism' affected respectively Spenser, Milton, Wordsworth, Shelley?

Point out how and to what extent the following works have been affected by the Italian Classics: Sackville's *Induction*, Shakespeare's *Venus and Adonis*, Milton's *Comus*, Gray's *Elegy*, Byron's *Don Juan*, Shelley's *Epipsychidion*, Tennyson's *In Memoriam*, Rossetti's *House of Life*.

> Describe the nature and extent of the direct influence of French
> Poetry on English Poetry during the Elizabethan age, noting
> especially Joachim du Bellay, Clement Marot, Robert Garnier, and
> Du Bartas.

> Lessing has remarked that 'Tragedy cannot take a step from the
> theory indicated by Aristotle without going precisely so far from
> perfection.' Discuss and illustrate that statement.[34]

Questions like these show Collins once again in a mood for
displaying his own breadth of reading and knowledge of literature—that tendency to show off which appeared in his delight in
recitation and retailing of literary facts. If these were intended as
actual examination questions then few people but Collins himself
could have tackled them. More likely, however, they were
intended to show sceptics like Freeman that literary study was
anything but a soft option, that it could be just as demanding as
philology. In practice, of course, even allowing for the fact that, in
Collins' utopian scheme, students would already have a solid basis
of classical literature behind them before coming on to the School
of Literature, major modifications would have to be made and
options introduced if the scheme was to be workable. It was a sad
let-down that after making out a convincing case for the study of
English literature in the universities, Collins should have been
driven to such ludicrous extremes.

Opinions of *The Study of English Literature* varied considerably at
the time. The *Saturday Review*, while it agreed with much of what
Collins had to say, objected to his 'Athanasius contra Mundum'
posture.[35] The *Spectator* primly remarked: 'We believe that the
cause of which he is so vigorous and well-equipped a champion is
essentially a good cause, but we think he would serve it even more
efficiently than he has done if he were at pains to modify the
sometimes almost forensic tone which characterises his methods of
advocacy.'[36] Not surprisingly, the most flattering review came
from the *University Extension Journal*, which remarked on the
'vigorous and fascinating' style of the book, and went on to say:

> The subject is one that lies very near to his heart—indeed, as
> thousands of grateful Extension students can testify, it has engaged
> the devotion of his best energies, through evil report and good
> report, for several generations of University life—and by his

thorough and scholarly handling of his theme he has proved his case to the hilt.[37]

Even those who disagreed with him had to admit that Collins as campaigner and dogged assembler of arguments was a force to be reckoned with.

4

The defeat of the Modern Languages proposal in November 1887 brought further demands for a new School at Oxford—this time an English School, where the competing interests of language and literature would, in theory, be harmonized.[38] In 1893, after protracted negotiations and consultations by interested parties at Oxford, Congregation finally decided in favour of an English School. After further discussions and amendments, the School received its final approval in Convocation in June 1894. There was a general air of satisfaction that the whole thing was settled once and for all and the Extension Movement was triumphant:

> The experience of University Extension workers long ago con-
> vinced them of the desirability of giving academic recognition to
> the study of English literature, and one of our lecturers, Mr
> Churton Collins, distinguished himself by faithful advocacy of the
> scheme at a time when it was much less popular than at present.[39]

But 'faithful advocacy' or not, the Oxford English School as set up in 1894 was not the School Collins had been fighting for. The first syllabus did contain three papers on later English literature up to 1832, but there were also five papers on Anglo-Saxon, Middle English, the history of the language and Gothic. A few compromises had been made in the favour of the literature men but the philologists overall had a firm grip on the syllabus. There was no reference to the Classics as Collins had insisted there must be.

Collins' own comments on the School came in an article in the *Nineteenth Century* in February 1895. As always on this topic, he made out a strongly-worded and convincing case. The School, as he rightly said, was an abortive compromise between a School of Philology and a School of Literature. The philological side was sound enough as far as it went and was 'the work of legislators who knew what they were about', but the literary side was pathetically inadequate: the set texts were a 'wretched farrago' and showed that there had been no coherent selection policy; very little attention was given to literary criticism, and none at all to the Classics. This meant from Collins' point of view (and surely from his Oxford supporters' point of view) that the School could never be seen as an Honours School of English Literature. With some modifications it might be turned into either a School of Philology or a Pass School of Literature, 'But no modification could make it into an Honour School of Literature correspondingly adequate, for the simple reason that the study of English literature cannot be isolated from the study of those literatures with which it is indissolubly linked.'[40] The last part of this showed Collins on his favourite obsession again but his main case against the Oxford English School was a fair one.

Collins' campaign, then, did not result in any major triumph for his own ideas and the new School represented a clear defeat for his English with Classics suggestion/insistence. This aside, however, he could look back on the period 1886–1894 with a certain satisfaction. He had established himself (at great cost to his personal relationships) as a hard-hitting reviewer easy-going literary men would need to be wary of; he had succeeded in turning a local Oxford issue into a national debate about the place of English literature in education; and he had done something to show that literary studies were not necessarily lightweight and trifling. Through his public campaign, he had also done something towards defeating the Modern Languages proposals in 1887: had this School been set up, English would have been a mere offshoot of Germanic philology and the English School of 1894 would never have emerged. Bad though it was in Collins' eyes, it was at least a School of English and might be improved later. Collins' appeals also had their role in persuading the University to create a chair of English *literature*. In June 1894, it was agreed to amalgamate the chairs of English and Anglo-Saxon at the next vacancy and to set up a chair of English literature with the available funds.[41]

Collins could also take satisfaction from his reputation in the Extension world, both in Britain and in the United States. In these circles, which cared nothing for the squabbles of the London literary world, he was seen as the ideal spokesman for literary education and a powerful propagandist for the Extension Movement's various interests. Collins was delighted when, in 1893, in recognition of his abilities and services, he was invited to lecture in the United States by the American Society for the Extension of University Teaching. He went there at the end of the year to find himself hailed as a hero by the American Extensionists. *Harper's Weekly*, for example, described him as follows:

> A modest and unaggressive man in private life, Mr Collins is a relentless foe to the medieval spirit in English education, and to the shameful neglect of aesthetic discipline and of the systematic study of English literature in the English universities. For the study of literature, not as a collection of grammatical exercises, not as a discussion of mooted points in philology, but as a clear expression of the life of a people, he is perhaps the strongest pleader today before the English-speaking world.[42]

Collins, who spent seven successful weeks lecturing in America,[43] must have been gratified to learn that, in some quarters at least, he was something other than a mere louse, Random Tearem, sour malcontent and general crank.

NOTES

1 University of Oxford Commission: *Minutes of Evidence*, 1881, pp. 9, 75, and 227–28.
2 *Oxford Magazine*, 27 October 1886, p. 309.
3 Walter Skeat, 'The Educational Value of English', *The Educational Review*, I, November 1891, p. 18.
4 E. M. W. Tillyard, *The Muse Unchained*, 1958, pp. 28 ff.
5 *Academy*, 23 January 1886, p. 61.
6 Ibid., 30 January 1886, p. 77.
7 Ibid., 13 February 1886, pp. 112–13, and 13 March, 1886, pp. 185–86.
8 The best known defences of literature at this time were by John Morley and Leslie Stephen. See respectively, Morley's lecture 'The Study of Literature', reprinted in *Studies in Literature*, 1890, pp. 189–228, and Stephen's article 'The Study of English Literature', *Cornhill*, May 1887, pp. 486–508.
9 *Pall Mall Gazette*, 22 October 1886, p. 1.

10 Ibid., 26 October 1886, pp. 1–2.

11 Ibid., 1 November 1886, p. 2.

12 Ibid., 27 November 1886, pp. 1–2.

13 Ibid., 2 December 1886, p. 5.

14 Ibid., 7 January 1887, pp. 1–2.

15 Jowett to Collins, letter dated 21 October 1886. Balliol College Library.

16 *Life and Letters of Benjamin Jowett*, ed. Evelyn Abbott and Lewis Campbell, 2 vols., 1897, II, 314–15.

17 J. C. Collins, 'Petition addressed to the Hebdomadal Council for the Foundation of a School of Modern Literature', *Quarterly Review*, CLXIV, January 1887, pp. 241–69.

18 *Oxford Magazine*, 19 January 1887, p. 8.

19 W. T. Stead was well known for his campaigns and crusades. See Phyllis Grosskurth, op. cit., pp. 282–83.

20 *Oxford Magazine*, 4 May 1887, pp. 174–75.

21 *Oxford University Gazette*, 26 April 1887, p. 381.

22 *Minutes of the Committee for University Extension*, June 1885–December 1889, p. 64. Bodleian Library.

23 Notebooks, 20 June 1887.

24 *The Times*, 5 May 1887, p. 11.

25 Ibid., 8 June 1887, p. 16.

26 Ibid., 5 May 1887, p. 11.

27 E. A. Freeman 'Literature and Language', *Contemporary Review*, LII, October 1887, pp. 549–67.

28 Ibid., p. 562.

29 See, for example, W. S. McCormick, *Three Lectures on English Literature*, Paisley, 1889, and John Nichol, *The Teaching of English Literature in our Universities and its Relation to Philology*, Liverpool, 1891.

30 L. C. Collins, op. cit., pp. 112–13.

31 J. C. Collins 'Can English Literature be Taught?', *Nineteenth Century*, XXII, November 1887, p. 642.

32 Ibid., pp. 644–45.

33 Ibid., p. 657.

34 J. C. Collins, *The Study of English Literature*, 1891, pp. 151–60.

35 *Saturday Review*, 2 January 1892, pp. 24–25.

36 *Spectator*, 5 March 1892, p. 334.

37 *University Extension Journal*, 15 February 1892, pp. 25–26.

38 See D. J. Palmer, op. cit., pp. 104 ff.

39 *Oxford University Extension Gazette*, June 1894, p. 108.

40 J. C. Collins, 'Language versus Literature at Oxford', *Nineteenth Century*, XXXVII, February 1895, pp. 290–303.

41 D. J. Palmer, op. cit., p. 112.
42 *Harper's Weekly*, 3 February 1894, p.114.
43 The only records of this visit which survive are to be found in L. C. Collins, op. cit., pp. 132–38.

CHAPTER SIX

THREE BOOKS

Further light is thrown on Collins' particular intentions and interests during the period 1891–95 by three books which he published at this time in addition to *The Study of English Literature*. Each of these books was an expanded version of lengthy articles published previously in journals—Collins' normal way of producing books—and each, in a different way, was clearly intended to show his credentials to the literary and educational worlds as a critic and scholar. As a strict and demanding reviewer of other people's work, he plainly felt the need to demonstrate in his own writings the kind of standards he was asking for. The three books in question here were *Illustrations of Tennyson* (1891), *Swift* (1893), and *Essays and Studies* (1895).

Illustrations of Tennyson was a version of articles which had originally appeared in the *Cornhill* in January and July 1880 and July 1881, and offered a new reading of the poet with the main emphasis on 'the nature and extent of his indebtedness to the writers who have preceded him'. In his new study of Tennyson Collins offered the literary world an alternative to comparative philology—comparative literature:

> Why so much importance should be attached to the comparative study of languages, and so little to the comparative study of literatures; why, in the interpretation of the masterpieces of poets, it should be thought necessary to accumulate parallels and illustrations of pecularities of syntax and grammar, and not be thought necessary to furnish parallels and illustrations of what is of far greater interest and importance, analogies namely in ideas, sentiments, modes of expression, and the like, whether arising from direct imitation, unconscious reminiscence, or similarity of temper and genius—the compiler of this little volume has never been able to understand.[1]

Collins, obviously enough, was not simply 'illustrating' Tennyson, he was also intent on showing the relatedness of classical and modern literature and how the study of the one must be brought into alliance with the other; in effect how the proper study of English literature demanded a knowledge and understanding of other literatures—precisely the case he made out the same year in *The Study of English Literature.*

When the first version of this study appeared in article form in 1880 Tennyson was furious. He had always been highly conscious of his relation to earlier poets and of his place within the literary tradition, but Collins with his endless citation of parallels and allusions seemed to be saying he was no more than a plagiarist—or, at best, a mere translator. His copy of the *Cornhill* containing Collins' first article is full of marginal denials and expostulations, some of them less than convincing.[2] Tennyson normally found it possible to keep on good terms with people he disagreed with, but he never forgave Collins for questioning the very thing he was touchiest about; his originality. Hence his scathing nickname for Collins as the louse on the locks of literature. Ten years later, in *Illustrations of Tennyson*, however, Collins had moderated his opinion slightly: Tennyson, like Virgil and Milton, was essentially an assimilative poet, sometimes consciously echoing others, sometimes simply drawing on a common store of thoughts and expressions, but in both cases—and this was the crucial point—improving what he used or borrowed. Tennyson, that is, was not a mere plagiarist or translator but a conscious craftsman able to use his borrowings creatively. It was a belated and half-hearted tribute to Tennyson the genius but Collins clearly felt the need to make some gesture at least in this direction.

Collins' studies of Tennyson were part of that long-term revaluation of his poetry which began during the later part of his life and continued well into the twentieth century; a revaluation which demoted him from the lofty position he enjoyed in his heyday and set him up as simply a gifted versifier. For Collins, Tennyson was precisely this; not 'a poet of great original genius' but an 'accomplished artist' seeing nature through the spectacles of art. Not that Collins was suggesting Tennyson's poetry therefore had no interest whatever; far from it. His poetry with its echoes of Homer, Virgil, Dante, and so on offered the discerning and cultivated reader an intellectual feast: 'to the scholar, and to the scholar alone, will his best and most characteristic works become in their full significance intelligible'.[3] Collins, in effect, was claiming to have discovered the real Tennyson in his researches; not the poet of broad popular appeal, the great public voice of Victorian England, but the scholarly, allusive poet—a poet after Collins' own heart—whose mass of borrowings he was delighted to be the first to point out and decode.

Collins argued that almost everything that Tennyson wrote owed something to some earlier writer. For example,

> Of his classical studies *Œnone* was modelled on the Theocritean Idylls; *Ulysses* and *Tithonus* on the soliloquies in the Greek plays. His *English Idylls* are obviously modelled on Theocritus, Southey and Wordsworth. In Wordsworth's *Michael* he found a model for *Enoch Arden*, and in Miss Procter's *Homeward Bound* the greater part of the plot. His *Lady Clare* was derived from Miss S. E. Ferrier's novel, *The Inheritance*. His *In Memoriam* was suggested by Petrarch; his *Dream of Fair Women* by Chaucer; his *Godiva* by Moultrie; his *Columbus* by Mr Ellis; the women's university in *The Princess* by Johnson. His *Lotos-Eaters* is an interpretative sketch from the *Odyssey*; his *Golden Supper* is from Boccaccio; his *Dora* is the versification of a story by Miss Mitford. His *Voyage of Madelune* is adapted from Joyce's *Celtic Romances*.[4]

Typical of Collins' assertiveness, there was no 'probably' or 'possibly' in all this, only certainty.

In his discussion of particular poems, Collins was able to draw on his vast store of literary quotations to indicate special instances of Tennyson's indebtedness to earlier writers. *Ulysses*, for example, was modelled not only on Greek sources but also on the twenty-sixth Canto of Dante's *Inferno* (94–126), which Collins quotes at length. But the poem also contains imitations from Homer 'too obvious to need specifying' (one example is cited), reminiscences from Horace, Teucer's speech to his comrades, *Odes*, I, vii. 24–32, and further echoes of Virgil, *Aeneid*, i. 748 and iii. 516.[5] However—Collins is anxious to stress this—Tennyson had not merely copied his sources: 'As is usual with him in all cases where he borrows, the details and minuter portions of the work are his own; he has added grace, elaboration, and symmetry ... A rough crayon draught has been metamorphosed into a perfect picture.'[6]

After working his way through a large selection of Tennyson's poems in this way, and having shown to his own satisfaction 'how indissolubly linked is the poetry of England with the poetry of the Greek, the Latin, and the Italian classics', Collins concluded by slightly qualifying his insistence on Tennyson's direct manipulating of earlier sources:

> Many analogies and parallels no doubt resolve themselves into mere coincidences; many are examples of those poetic commonplaces which must necessarily abound wherever poetry finds voluminous expression; but the greater part of them as obviously represent the material on which he has worked as the Homeric parodies in the *Aeneid* indicate their originals.[7]

This was a slight concession to Tennyson's originality perhaps, though obviously Collins intended his main case for borrowings to stand.

In his desire to see English and European literature forming a whole network of inter-connexions, Collins was unfailingly dogmatic on the issue of literary indebtedness; nor did he feel he was casting a slur on Tennyson's reputation by describing him as a skilful imitator and borrower—far from it. As time passed, he devoted much of his critical effort to establishing various cases of indebtedness between writers and speculated about many more. His favourite questions included such things as 'had Shakespeare read the Greek Classics?', 'Was the author of Beowulf acquainted with the Iliad?' and in his keenness to answer such questions in the affirmative he often offered dubious evidence to support his case. But where Tennyson was concerned at least, Collins was on much firmer ground. Tennyson, it was agreed, was a deliberate poetic craftsman, fascinated by traditional conventions, forms and metres, extremely well versed in classical and European literature, and a conscious imitator in much of his poetry. Collins was probably wrong in particular instances when suggesting parallels and sources but his general view of Tennyson the literary craftsman was convincing enough. Tennyson in the end seems to have admitted as much and after violently rejecting some of Collins' attributions in 1880 with an outright 'no' later quietly slipped the same references into later editions of his poetry.[8] Collins, for his part, continued to admire Tennyson precisely for his literary allusiveness and later edited selections of his poetry.

Illustrations of Tennyson was hailed as a brilliant *tour de force* when it appeared in 1891—it was the first time Tennyson had been given the exhaustive treatment usually reserved for classical poets. The *Spectator*, for instance, remarked, 'The spirit in which Mr Collins enters on his work is excellent, and what he writes is throughout distinguished by fine scholarship . . . As an incentive to the study of all poetry, Mr Collins' book has very real value.'[9] The *Echo* went even further: 'No critical reader of Tennyson can afford to dispense with it. . . Mr Collins' book is a credit to English scholarship. As a study of Tennyson it is unique; it opens a new field of literary criticism.' Collins, that is to say, was doing for comparative literary studies what the Sweets and Müllers were doing for comparative philology. Others, however, were more doubtful. Collins' approach to Tennyson was doubtless learned and meticulous but it mainly served to show up the difference between a 'critic' and a mere 'commentator'. Richard Le Gallienne, writing on behalf of the aesthetic critics, made this very point in his review of the book. Collins had a 'prodigious memory' and was expert in discovering allusions but he scarcely conveyed the real essence of Tennyson's poetry to his readers. To Le Gallienne the real question for the critic was:

> Does this poetry give me the sense of a new personality, present as a new magic, of rhythm or what not, in the verse? If so, one need trouble no further, and we can with indifference watch the commentator, like a demon-mole, burrowing his way in his little tunnels of learning beneath the text.[10]

Collins later caught up with Le Gallienne when he reviewed some of his literary tastings: 'Whatever be his theme, poem, essay, novel, picture, he contrives to serve it up with the same condiment, a sickly and nauseous compound of preciosity and sentimentalism.'[11] Le Gallienne, however, provided a view of Collins the industrious source-hunter (demon-mole rather than louse this time) which was generally shared by the writers of the nineties: his chief talent was for spotting literary connexions and influences—some genuine, some spurious—rather than for subtle and sympathetic readings of the text.

2

Collins' next book, *Jonathan Swift: a Biographical and Critical Study*, published in 1893, was based on two articles which appeared earlier in the *Quarterly* in April 1882 and July 1883. This work was a return to the sort of study Collins had produced of Bolingbroke and Voltaire in 1886—in other words a work of literary history and biographical revaluation. Collins' interest in Swift, as was often the case with him, came from his sense of the man as a misunderstood and much maligned figure; someone who was partly the victim of his own character but even more so of his biographers. Justice had to be done and a fair assessment made and this, of course, was very much to Collins' taste. There was not much new biographical and historical material around by the 1880s but Collins was eager to offer his own ideas and speculations on a well-researched area.

Collins began in his usual manner reviewing previous work on Swift with some typically outspoken comments. Scott's memoir was 'essentially unthorough', 'the work of a man, of a very great man, who was contented with doing respectably what with a little more trouble he might have done excellently'. John Forster's unfinished *Life of Jonathan Swift* (1875) might have been the definitive biography, but unfortunately remained only a 'fragment'; moreover it was marred by its diffuseness and its failure to distinguish between the important and the unimportant: 'Nothing that Swift did or said was in his estimation too unimportant to be chronicled. He pounced with ludicrous avidity on matter which was not merely worthless in itself, but of no value in its bearings on Swift.' Finally, there was Henry Craik's *Life of Jonathan Swift* (1882), a work with which Collins could find no fault: Craik had written accurately, skilfully, and intelligently and had used new material unavailable to previous biographers.[12] Craik perhaps had left Collins little to say about Swift—he belonged to that select band of literary critics and historians (Arnold, Mark Pattison, Leslie Stephen, W. J. Courthope and Sidney Lee among them) for whom Collins had nothing but praise. However, there were one or two important readjustments to be made to the general picture of Swift and his works.

Collins' book on Swift is one of his more serious and responsible contributions to literary history and criticism, with none of the extraneous propagandist intentions of books like *Illustrations of Tennyson* and *The Study of English Literature* which, for all their learning and force, were too closely allied to his campaign for uniting English and Classics to be fully convincing. Like other nineteenth-century writers on Swift, Collins attempted to correct the popular view of him as a 'gloomy' and 'ferocious misanthrope', 'with a heart of stone and a tongue of poison'. This was the image of Swift perpetuated by Macaulay and Thackeray and only partially countered by more objective biographers like Forster and Craik. Interestingly, Collins, the 'new Macaulay', strongly objects to Macaulay's description of Swift as 'the apostate politician, the ribald priest, the perjured lover, the heart burning with hatred against the whole human race'. The rhetoric might remind one of Collins' at particular moments, but here Collins distances himself from it, and similarly rejects Thackeray's famous diatribe on Swift in *English Humorists of the Eighteenth Century* (1853). For Thackeray, Swift, at least in Book IV of *Gulliver's Travels*, was 'a monster gibbering shrieks, and gnashing imprecations against mankind'; for Collins, Thackeray's judgment was 'shallow', 'flashy' and 'unjust', betraying an extraordinary ignorance of Swift's character and an unwarrantable slur on his reputation.[13]

The main part of the book carefully traces the various stages of Swift's career and writings. The main themes are Swift's 'honesty and sincerity' as a politician and churchman; his 'morbidity of temperament' which fatally complicated his relationship with women; his courageous efforts to confront the Irish problem ('It fevered his blood, it broke his rest, it drove him at times half-frantic with furious indignation'); and his sense of failure: 'So far from having derived any gratification either from his recent triumph or from the discharge of duty, he continued to be, what in truth he had long been, the most wretched, the most discontented, the most solitary of men.'[14] This last comment suggests the kind of fellow-feeling which drew Collins to Swift in the first place; Collins' situation was of course more hopeful than Swift's, but already by the 1880s he was beginning to feel similarly un-rewarded for all his effort and honesty.

Despite his defence of Swift's career, and in part of his character, Collins could scarcely ignore his savage view of mankind as it appeared in his writings, and especially in *Gulliver*. Although Collins had dismissed Thackeray's judgment of Swift as shallow and distorted, in his account of *Gulliver* he was forced to concede something to him. *Gulliver*, Collins agreed, showed a hatred and contempt for mankind far from satirical:

> Where satire has a moral purpose it is discriminating. It is levelled, not at defects and infirmities which are essential and in nature unremovable, but at defects and infirmities which are unessential, and therefore corrigible. If its immediate object is to punish, its ultimate object is to amend. But this is not the spirit of *Gulliver*. Take the Yahoos. Nothing can be plainer than that those odious and repulsive creatures were designed to be types, not of man, as man when brutalised and degenerate may become, but of man as man is naturally constituted.'[15]

Collins, however, emphasizes the differences between the last two books of *Gulliver* and the first two, where the humour, though often pungent, is seldom bitter. In the last two books 'Swift's design began and ended in cynical mockery.'[16]

So Collins, finally, has to agree that many of Swift's later writings, including the poems, contain 'the very alcohol of hatred and contempt'. Yet this he argues is not sufficient reason for accepting the sweeping dismissive verdicts of Macaulay and Thackeray. Swift's later writings were the expression of a wretched and disappointed man who nevertheless, in his private and public life, was charitable and just: 'The most savage of misanthropes was in practice the most indefatigable of philanthropists . . . Indeed, no one who deserved assistance or needed advice ever applied to him in vain.'[17] In other words, like Craik, Collins argues that a distinction needs to be drawn between Swift the man and Swift the writer, and further distinctions drawn between the different writings, if a proper critical estimate is to be made. The author of the last two books of *Gulliver* might sound like a gibbering monster, but Swift himself is a more complicated matter.

Collins' chief sympathy for Swift the man is felt in his account of his final years as his infirmities increased and his mind began to fail:

> Into a particular account of Swift's last years it would be almost agony to enter. Nothing in the recorded history of humanity,

nothing that the imagination of man has conceived, can transcend
in horror and pathos the accounts which have come down to us of
the closing scenes of his life.[18]

Allowing for some characteristic overstatement here, Collins was
obviously powerfully moved by Swift's final degradation and
pain. As time passed, Collins often speculated with much horror
about his own end, jotting down his fears in his private notebooks—this being the case, he was not surprisingly drawn by
morbid curiosity into a contemplation of Swift's decline into
disease and imbecility.

In connexion with this interest, or anxiety, Collins was eager to
dispose of the popular idea that Swift was the victim of a disease
which ultimately developed into insanity—that is, that his so-
called 'madness' was a gradual growth. This idea had already been
refuted in 1846 by Sir William Wilde in the *Dublin Quarterly Journal
of Medical Science*, but Collins went through the subject again, with
the assistance of a Dr Bucknill, whose evidence he published as an
Appendix to his book. On the best medical evidence, Swift
certainly suffered from a number of serious ailments but these
were not responsible for his eventual dementia and aphasia, which
probably came about as the result of a stroke. Swift's mind, Collins
insisted, remained sane and clear, until well into his seventies:

> The truth is that a mind saner than Swift's, a mind of stouter and
> stronger fabric, a mind in which the reason, the pure reason, sate
> enthroned more securely has never existed. From first to last, so
> long as he continued in possession of his faculties, it was his
> distinguishing characteristic; it was his standard; it was his touch-
> stone; it remained unshaken and unimpaired, a fortress of rock on
> which the turbulent chaos of his furious passions broke harm-
> lessly.[19]

This might well have been the case, yet obviously there is a special
urgency in Collins' insistence here; an urgency related to the
worries and complexes which darkened his own life.[20]

Having asserted Swift's sanity as strongly as he could, Collins
then moved on to a final assessment of the man. Swift, he argued,
was basically the victim of 'opposite natures' within the one
temperament. He was sensitive and kind and outraged by injustice, but he was utterly devoid of 'a sense of the beautiful in

nature, in the human form, in morals, in art, in philosophy'; he had no perception of the ideal, or the religious. He was excessively rational and utilitarian in outlook and never seems to have had 'even a glimpse of those truths which lie outside the scope of the senses and the reason, and which find their expression in poetry and in sentimental religion.' 'In his estimate of life and the world generally he saw everything in the clear cold light of the pure intellect.' Swift inevitably brought Hobbes to mind: 'pessimists and cynics by both temper and conviction, they were deficient in all those instincts and sympathies on which every true estimate and every true philosophy must be based'.[21]

Like a good many critics from Johnson to Leavis, Collins was obviously both sympathetic to and repelled by Swift. Swift had great intellectual powers but lacked human depth and soul; his intelligence was always working within strict limits:

> The sphere within which his intelligence worked and within which his sympathy and insight were bounded was, comparatively speaking, a narrow one. He had the eye of a lynx for all that moves on the surface of life and for all that may be found on the beaten highway of commonplace experience, but the depths he neither explored nor perhaps even suspected.[22]

In the end Collins' sympathetic view of Swift is heavily undercut by his Carlylean sense of his defects—his cynicism, his lack of idealism, his religious scepticism. He is only moved to sympathy for Swift when thinking of his personal problems, his sensitivity and pride, his last sufferings, and the tragic waste of genius brought about by his character and circumstances. Swift in other words was another of those Collinsian tragic figures, his immense gifts and energy 'now frittering themselves away on trifles, now roused for a moment to concentrated action by passion, interest, or benevolence, but never assuming their true proportions, never developing into full activity'.[23]

As with Bolingbroke earlier, Collins' study of Swift was chiefly notable for its striking portrait of the man. Chapter X of the book is an extended and brilliantly pointed portrait of Swift, though it has its almost inevitable Macaulayesque exaggerations and simplifications, showing once again Collins' zest for probing the psychology of genius and his fascination with its conflicts and self-cancellations. Otherwise the book added little that was new to the subject and to some extent stood in the shadow of other studies— notably Henry Craik's and Leslie Stephen's both published in 1882 (by coincidence—or perhaps not—both Craik and Stephen were referees for Collins when he applied for university posts). All the same, Collins had shown himself to be a lively biographer and critic once again and his book survived his own time[24] even finding its place in the 'still useful' category in modern bibliographies.[25]

3

Hard pressed by Extension commitments, his campaigns and educational writings, Collins was nevertheless still ambitious to produce more scholarly work and in May 1893 discussed with Macmillan a proposal for a History of England in several volumes from the accession of George I to 1789.[26] This was similar to the proposal discussed with Rivington back in 1880 and, like that project, came to nothing. Collins through the pressure of his other work was never in a position to write the sequel to Macaulay's History he would like to have written. Macmillan, however, did bring out his *Essays and Studies* in 1895, which included articles on Dryden, The Predecessors of Shakespeare, Chesterfield, Theobald and Menander which had previously appeared in journals. Three of the articles demonstrated Collins' interest in the Augustans (the period his History was to have been concerned with) and the collection as a whole was designed as an exercise in scholarly and impartial criticism—yet another reassertion of critical standards 'against the mischievous tendencies of the New School of Criticism, a school as inimical to good taste and good sense as it is to morals and decency'.[27] Collins' inclusion of the review of Symonds' book on Shakespeare's predecessors with its scathing comments on Swinburne gave extra polemical weight to his case.

It is plain from a reading of *Essays and Studies* the main reason why Collins was attracted to the Augustans was that he felt that they stood for literary and critical standards his own age was fast losing sight of—they could therefore be enlisted in his fight against the dilettantes and aesthetes. Here Dryden was the key figure (the Matthew Arnold, if not the Churton Collins of his time):

> He had determined the bent of a great literature at a great crisis. He had banished for ever the unpruned luxuriance, the licence, the essentially uncritical spirit, which had marked expression in the literature of Elizabeth and James, and he had vindicated the substitution of a style which should proceed on critical principles, which should aim at terseness, precision and point, should learn to restrain itself, should master the mysteries of selection and suppression . . . He had brought home to us the masterpieces of the Roman Classics, and he had taught us how to understand and interpret them.[28]

There was nothing basically new in this view of Dryden's role as writer and critic: what was new was Collins' tendentious use of Dryden to support his own case against late Victorian 'unpruned luxuriance' and 'licence'. Arnold up to his death in 1888 had been the nearest equivalent to Dryden in the fight for critical standards; what was needed now in the mid-nineties—in the absence of a new Dryden or Arnold—was a concerted effort by serious-minded critics and reviewers to trounce the whole breed of aesthete-critics and reassert the best classical standards. Collins himself, very evidently, was happy to take a leading role in this campaign for sound criticism and cool judgment, though most readers questioned whether his Macaulayesque talents really equipped him for the position.

Collins provides a clear survey of Dryden's life and writings, following the lines of his chief editors Walter Scott (*Life and Works of John Dryden*, 18 vols., 1821) and W. D. Christie (*The Poetical Works of John Dryden*, 1870), but offers his own sharp opinions on the man. At such moments Collins always brought his own private feelings to the fore, and he had some strong points to make about Dryden the man of letters. Dryden, for example, in later life complained of great hardships and struggles, yet Collins mindful of his own problems, remarks: 'He complains bitterly of his poverty, and poor he undoubtedly was; yet he never could have wanted the necessaries of life . . . He complains of the malice of his enemies, and yet he might have solaced himself by remembering his friends, for he could number among them some of the most illustrious, the most hospitable, and the most charming of his contemporaries.'[29] Dryden, that is to say, knew nothing of the hardships of lesser writers and critics whose life was one long struggle for recognition. Despite this personal note, Collins' Dryden essay was praised by contemporary reviewers—including Saintsbury, by this time an authority on Dryden[30]—as a model of exposition and clear summation.

The essays on Chesterfield and Theobald were exercises in rehabilitation. Chesterfield's character, like Swift's in Collins' view, had been maligned by the critics: 'his name is little more than a synonym for a profligate fribble, shallow, flippant, heartless, without morality, without seriousness, a scoffer at religion, an enemy to truth and virtue, passing half his life in practising, and the other half in teaching a son to practise, all that moves loathing and contempt in honest men'.[31] Collins' essay—following Lord Carnarvon's lead in his edition of Chesterfield's letters in 1890— shows by reference to other of his writings that Chesterfield had much better qualities than had been recognized. Like Dryden, Chesterfield was a model for the late nineteenth century in literary critical terms: 'We need the corrective—the educational corrective—of his refined good sense, his measure, his sobriety, his sincerity, his truthfulness, his instinctive application of artistocratic standards in attainment, of aristocratic touchstones in criticism.'[32] Chesterfield was of interest then partly because his reputation needed some repair-work but much more so because he exemplified standards Collins approved of. This explains Collins' resuscitation of an almost forgotten figure whose worldly hauteur he doubtless disliked. Perhaps too, he saw something of his own complex personality in Chesterfield's. Writing of some of Chesterfield's less well-known letters, he commented 'They show how much amiability, kindliness, humanity, seriousness, existed in one whose name has become a proverb for the very opposite qualities.'[33] Precisely the same contradictions of course bedevilled Collins' own reputation.

The essay on Theobald was another typical piece of Collinsian rehabilitation. Theobald, known almost exclusively as Pope's chief dunce in the *Dunciad*, was for Collins a tragic figure. A scholar of great abilities, lacking proper recognition, he was forced to scribble feeble plays and poems to keep himself and his family from starvation and in doing so enabled his enemies 'to make havoc of his reputation'. Again not exactly a Churton Collins, but there are similarities. Theobald, in Collins' view, was not simply a great Shakespearean editor but—more to the point—a scholar after his own heart: 'His notes are, indeed, a storehouse of the most felicitous illustrations of Shakespeare's images, sentiments, and thoughts, drawn from the whole range of the Greek and Roman classics, illustrations which have been appropriated without a word of acknowledgement by succeeding generations of commentators.'[34] This of course was Collins' own specialty, already taken up in his study of Tennyson, and later pursued into Theobald's own territory in the researches which took shape in his *Studies in Shakespeare* (1904).

Two years after *Essays and Studies*, Collins wrote to Sidney Lee asking if he might write an article on Theobald for the *Dictionary of National Biography*:

> I think that I have established Theobald's claim to rank very much higher than he is supposed to rank, as a critic and commentator; but as the essay in which I have done this in my 'Essays and Studies'— 'The Porson of Shakespearean Criticism' will probably pass, probably already has passed into oblivion, I should like for poor Theobald's sake to do him justice in a place which will certainly defy oblivion.[35]

Collins' probably had more selfish reasons too for wanting to write an article for the *Dictionary of National Biography*, but one feels that he really did want to do justice to a fellow-scholar and Grub Street struggler like Theobald, the Churton Collins of his day. Collins' article was accepted by Lee for the *Dictionary of National Biography* where it remains as a standing rebuke to the view of Theobald put forward by the *Encyclopedia Britannica* which Collins cites:

> Theobald will survive as the prime butt of the original Dunciad . . . He was a man with literary impulses, but without genius, even of a superficial kind. As a student, as a commentator, he might have led a happy and enviable life, had not the vanity of the literary idea led him into a false position.[36]

Collins, identifying too closely with Theobald, and reacting against this bleak verdict, no doubt goes too far in the other direction by way of revaluation.

The final chapter of *Essays and Studies* deals with Menander and is based on one of Collins' earliest articles published in the *Cornhill* in May 1879. Menander, the Greek comic dramatist, whose surviving fragments of plays were admired by Goethe and Arnold, is the odd man out in *Essays and Studies*. He has no obvious relation to the other figures in the book and offers few points of contact with Collins' other interests, apart from his passion for anything Greek. The essay consists chiefly of short quotations from Menander—there being little else to discuss—with Collins' own translations and was probably intended to demonstrate his skill as a commentator on Greek literature to a journal-reading public that in 1879 was only just beginning to hear of Churton Collins. Its reappearance in a book, the main purpose of which is to use particular writers in support of Collins' running argument with the Victorian age, remains a mystery unless it was intended as another pointer to his own impeccable good taste.

Essays and Studies was generally well-received in 1895, though as always in reviews of Collins' works there were the usual doubts and dislikes. The *Saturday Review*, for example, made the following typical assessment of the book:

> Mr Collins occupies a distinguished place of his own among contemporary critics of literature. He has opinions and dares to give them uncompromising expression; he has energy; he has learning; he asserts authority; he maintains a tradition ... but he treats his authors less as a lover than as a judge; he dreads extravagance of the emotions; he does not lie down to repose, to browse, to ruminate; he toils, investigates, accumulates, arranges, pronounces.[37]

Saintsbury, too, found *Essays and Studies* an 'interesting', 'learned' and 'energetic' book but also found fault with Collins' old-style 'opinionatedness'. Collins was a respected critic, that is to say, but his remorseless judicial method together with what Saintsbury called his lack of 'ease', 'springiness' and 'unction' reminded readers of an earlier generation of critical judges (the Jeffreys and Macaulays) whose approach was out of vogue. 'The older fashion', said Saintsbury, 'was not ostensibly to give the critic's personal warranty, but to assume that his opinion was that of the *orbis terrarum*, that there was no possibility of salvation outside of it, and that anybody who did not choose to accept it ought to be delivered over to the secular arm'.[38] Collins, however, obviously felt that there was more than enough springiness and unction in contemporary critical writing and was eager to distance himself from the self-indulgences of the Swinburnes and Gosses by adopting as categorical and assertive a manner as possible (though of course his own temperamental fondness for this style came into it as well). His opinionatedness, too, which was the expression of deeply held convictions, also had the virtue of giving his writings a force not to be found in those of springier writers like Saintsbury, though this very forcefulness at times was plainly counter-productive since readers soon wearied of his massive barrage of words when he was driving his favourite themes. Hence the mixed response to *Essays and Studies*: it was a lively, learned book, but too extreme in what was now recognized as the familiar Collinsian fashion. In retrospect, *Essays and Studies* in fact has an air of pathos about it; a sense of Collins fighting one more losing battle as well as merely touching on literary topics he never found the opportunity to develop.

NOTES

1 J. C. Collins, *Illustrations of Tennyson*, 1891, p. v.
2 For a discussion of this and related issues, see Robert Pattison, *Tennyson and Tradition*, Cambridge, Massachusetts, 1979, Chapter I.
3 *Illustrations of Tennyson*, p.viii.
4 Ibid., pp. 7–8.
5 Ibid., p. 58–59.
6 Ibid., p. 58.
7 Ibid., pp. 176–77.
8 Robert Pattison, op. cit., p. 7.
9 Extracts from these two reviews were printed in Collins' book on Swift in 1893 as part of the advertisement for *Illustrations of Tennyson*.
10 Richard Le Gallienne, *Retrospective Reviews*, I, 1891–93, pp. 19–28.
11 See J. C. Collins, *Ephemera Critica*, p. 155. Le Gallienne, poet, critic, contributor to the *Yellow Book* and writer of charming fantasies and romances, for Collins represented the aesthetic movement at its most affected and decadent, though he allowed him some intelligence and ability. Oscar Wilde would have been the obvious target for Collins' dislike of the aesthetes but for some reason he never mentions him.
12 J. C. Collins, *Jonathan Swift*, 1893, pp. 5–10.

13   Ibid., p. 16.
14   Ibid., pp. 67, 75, 167 and 194.
15   Ibid., p. 209.
16   Ibid., p. 209.
17   Ibid., pp. 231–32.
18   Ibid., p. 235.
19   Ibid., 241.
20   See above, p. 54.
21   *Swift*, pp. 242–49.
22   Ibid., p. 264.
23   Ibid., p. 255.
24   See for example the brief references to Collins' book in F. R. Leavis, *The Common Pursuit*, 1962, p. 74, and in Michael Foot's introduction to the Penguin edition of *Gulliver's Travels*, 1967, pp. 14–15.
25   See for example the Norton Critical Edition of *Gulliver's Travels*, ed. Robert A. Greenberg, New York, 1961, p. 358.
26   L. C. Collins, op. cit., p. 131.
27   J. C. Collins, *Essays and Studies*, p. viii.
28   Ibid., pp. 1–2.
29   Ibid., p. 72.
30   *The Bookman*, March 1895, pp. 178–79.
31   *Essays and Studies*, p. 195.
32   Ibid., p. 262.
33   Ibid., p. 196.
34   Ibid., p. 311.
35   L. C. Collins, op. cit., p. 144.
36   *Essays and Studies*, p. 275.
37   *Saturday Review*, 16 March 1895, pp. 353–54.
38   *The Bookman*, March 1895, p. 178.

CHAPTER SEVEN

THE 'SATURDAY' REVIEWER

In 1895, when *Essays and Studies* came out, Collins was at the mid-point of his career and could look back over the previous fifteen years or so with mixed feelings. He was well-established in the University Extension world both as a teacher and propagandist; on the other hand in order to carry out all his lecturing commitments—which he was always adding to—and pursue his literary researches, article writing and reviewing, he was forced to drive himself at a furious pace. L. C. Collins gives an example of a typical week's work at this time which indicates the kind of pressures he habitually worked under:

Sunday—Article for *Saturday Review* on O. Morgan's 'Eclogues of Virgil' (appeared following Saturday).

Monday—Lecture at Surbiton on Byron's 'Childe Harold'; at Richmond on Tennyson's 'Idylls'; at Toynbee Hall on Aeschylus.

Tuesday—Lecture at Miss Geach's on Virgil's 'Aeneid'; at Miss Spark's on Chaucer's 'Canterbury Tales'; at Westbourne Park Institute on Macaulay; at City of London College on 'King Lear'.

Wednesday—Two lectures at Levana House, Wimbledon, on Elizabeth's Reign and on Euripides' 'Medea'; lecture at 92 Eaton Terrace on Landor; at New Cross on Landor's Life.

Thursday—Lecture at Brondesbury on Elizabeth's Reign; at 13 Thurloe Square on Addison; at Bromley on Aeschylus' 'Prometheus'; at Battersea Polytechnic on 'Cymbeline'.

Friday—Lecture at Hayward's Heath on the 'Iliad'; at Brighton on 'Childe Harold'; on Swift; on Milton.

Saturday—Lecture at Kenilworth, Clapham Common, on Browning's 'La Saisiaz'.

Sunday (with part of Saturday)—Opinion for Arnold on a MS.
Dante at Ravenna and Duke of Guise, a Tragedy; article
on Skrine's Poems.
Dinner Party on Saturday—Watts, Sidney Lee, and Mumm;
correspondence also on Sunday.[1]

Even granting the fact that Collins in many cases here would have
been repeating lectures already given several times before, the
sheer range and volume of work together with the non-stop move
from place to place dramatically suggests why he always seemed to
be on the brink of crisis.

2

This pressure and pace far from slackening in the late 1890s
increased when Collins was invited by Frank Harris to write on a
regular basis for the *Saturday Review*. Harris had just taken over the
editorship of the *Saturday* and was determined to make it a
provocative and outspoken journal once again after its period of
decline. It says much for Collins' reputation that he was one of the
first reviewers, along with H. G. Wells and George Bernard Shaw,
to be invited on to the staff. From 1894 to 1906, Collins wrote
regularly for the *Saturday* and found in it just the platform he was
looking for: in the *Saturday* he could berate the universities and the
literary world to his heart's content, continue his old campaigns,
send out appeals, and follow up all his interests with strong
editorial backing.

Frank Harris met Collins shortly after his attack on Gosse in
1886 and was agreeably impressed by him. As he later described
him,

> Churton Collins was some five feet eight inches or nine in height, a
> strong, square figure, not particularly muscular, though he was a
> fair walker and cyclist. The head was of good shape and size, the
> forehead broad, the eyes pale blue, the jaw and chin peculiarly
> square and massive. Considerable brain-power one would have
> said, and very considerable determination.[2]

Harris was struck by Collins' honesty, kindliness, 'chivalry and
loyalty' and noted both his 'extraordinary reverence for facts' and

his 'incomprehensible bitterness towards what he regarded as pretentious ignorance'. Oddly, though, he claimed Collins suffered from a bad memory for verse!

Collins' main targets in the *Saturday* were the by this time familiar ones of the aesthetic movement, literary cliques, the universities, and careless Gosse-like scholarship. He quickly established himself as a sharp no-nonsense reviewer in November and December 1894 with three lethal notices of Clarendon Press editions: Thomas Arnold's edition of Dryden's *Essay of Dramatic Poesy* he showed to be merely superficial; Aldis Wright's edition of *Hamlet* he argued was far too philologically-minded and pedantic; and W. M. Rossetti's edition of Shelley's *Adonais* he found wanting in its lack of awareness of the classical influence on Shelley.[3] Each review, of course, was part of his long-term attack on the universities—and particularly Oxford—for their neglect of key issues in English literary studies and for their preference for philology over literature. Collins, however, as usual did not simply assert these failings in the books concerned, he supported his case by detailed quotation and argument in his best judicial manner. These first reviews, moreover, had some effect; readers sat up and took notice of them. Arnold's edition, correspondents suggested, was not really a typical specimen of Oxford editing, and Rossetti was generous enough to accept Collins' criticism and later had his edition of *Adonais* revised by someone with greater classical knowledge than himself.[4] Being reviewed by Collins was clearly a disturbing experience.

Collins' next important review was on the lines of his attack on Gosse and brought him into conflict with someone who was prepared to answer back. It was a review of J. J. Jusserand's *Literary History of the English People from the Origins to the Renaissance* and was entitled 'A Gallop through English Literature'.[5] Collins was an admirer of certain French critics, Taine and Sainte-Beuve included, but his admiration stopped well short of Jusserand's *Literary History*. The review opens with the ironic Macaulayesque remark that 'There is a breeziness and hilarity, a gay irresponsibility and abandon about M. Jusserand which is perfectly delightful. He is the very Autolycus of History and Criticism. What more sober students, who have some conscience to trouble them, are "toiling all their lives to find" appears to be his as a sort of natural right.' Jusserand, in other words, was precisely the sort of scholar Collins detested—the easy and careless skimmer who knew nothing of the pains authors like Collins suffered.

Collins' bantering opening flourish soon gave way to a more earnest tone in the body of the review. The first part of Jusserand's book dealt superficially with subjects covered far more effectively by Ten Brink and Henry Morley; the section on Chaucer was much better, but on the uncharted areas of fourteenth and fifteenth-century literature, he had been led astray by unreliable guides: he 'actually tells us that Gower's *Speculum Meditantis* is lost!' Ignoring the possible defence that the book was only meant for a popular readership, Collins reprimanded Jusserand for his slackness: 'Now we would ask M. Jusserand in all seriousness, what possible end can be served by a book of this kind, except the encouragement of everything that is abhorrent to the real scholar: superficiality, want of thoroughness, and false assumption, and what is more, the public dissemination of error, and of crude and misleading judgments.' Collins, however, overstepped the mark in this instance in his eagerness to find another Gossian victim. Jusserand was a better scholar than Collins' review gave him credit for and when it was republished in *Ephemera Critica* he defended himself with some ability in the *Revue Critique*.[6] Collins, always on the watch for shoddy scholarship, was liable to make mountains out of molehills and in more than one case laid himself open to the charge of pernicketiness.

He was on safer ground with Gosse, again, whose *Short History of Modern English Literature* (1898) showed the same faults as his earlier volumes—'There is not a chapter in the book which does not teem with errors'—and with that other omnipresent figure of the late Victorian literary journals, George Saintsbury.[7] Saintsbury, a rival to Collins in the sphere of book consumption, was the most prolific of the late Victorian scholar-critics, producing enough books, articles, reviews and miscellaneous pieces over a lifetime to fill a hundred large volumes. As a comparative failure at Oxford, and as a teacher and journalist, his career had its obvious parallels with Collins', and Collins, who knew him slightly, certainly regarded him as a rival. This was especially so after 1895, when Saintsbury was appointed to the Chair of Rhetoric and English Literature at Edinburgh; a post which

Collins had his eye on.[8] Saintsbury was undeniably another demon-mole, covering vast fields in his researches and writings, but, unlike Collins, he was an amazingly undisciplined writer, highly subjective and impressionistic and to some degree under the influence of the Art for Art's sake movement. Not least of all, accuracy was one of his weaker points and he wrote carelessly and often muddled his dates. All in all, he was a critic of the very opposite type from Collins (whose work he nonetheless reviewed generously) and so represented a threat to Collins' idea of critical standards. Edinburgh chair or no Edinburgh chair, he would certainly have come into Collins' line of fire sooner or later, but the Edinburgh appointment obviously sharpened Collins' responses when he read Saintsbury's books.

Collins' first review of Saintsbury's work came in November 1895[9] and dealt with his *Essays in English Literature 1780–1860*. The review made it plain that Saintsbury's university appointment was the main focus of interest. It was headed 'A Professor of English Literature on his own Subject' and opened with the ominous comment: 'Here men of letters and students of English literature may fairly expect to find the qualifications that must exist to justify Professor Saintsbury's appointment, the great excellences that must have been required to outweigh the claims of such a teacher of English literature as Mr Churton Collins, or so inspiring a critic of it as Mr W. E. Henley.' (In writing an unsigned review, Collins did not scruple about using his own name for polemical purposes.) The essays of course were a gift to the reviewer; they were negligently written, had no real coherence (Collins called them an 'ephemeral farrago', one of his favourite abusive terms), and were full of mistakes: 'in simple matters of fact and chronology, Professor Saintsbury stands sorely in need of the teaching it is now his duty to impart to the students of Edinburgh University'.[10] Saintsbury had been careless with many of his facts and dates, but the review was obviously out to make the most of the smallest trifles. Saintsbury, for example, speaking of Strutt's *Queenhoo Hall*, had inadvertently said 'the book is a very rare one'; Collins immediately pounced: 'If Professor Saintsbury had read the General Preface to Waverley he would have known that Strutt left the work in MS ... It is not a rare book; it simply does not exist.' Thus the 'Professor' was made to look the complete incompetent;

at least that was the intention, but Collins was so manifestly unfair and quibbling over minute details that his broader and more reasonable case against scholarly carelessness was in danger of getting lost.

Saintsbury's position at Edinburgh gave him a special prominence in Collins' eye, but his reaction to Saintsbury's work was also provoked by the respect with which this work was treated by other reviewers and authors. Richard Garnett in his *Age of Dryden* (1895), for example, praised the work of Saintsbury and Gosse (and Collins too!) in his preface and brought Collins' anger down on himself for participating in the pernicious game of log-rolling by which false reputations were set up.[11] Saintsbury, then, became associated in Collins' eyes with the literary cliques who foisted pretentious and erroneous works on to gullible readers, and he kept a sharp eye out for new Saintsbury productions.

His next book, *A History of Nineteenth Century Literature* (1896) was reviewed by Collins under the heading 'A Blind Guide in Victorian Literature'.[12] Like the other book, this one was full of mistakes large and small, together with more debatable matters, such as the question of particular influences on Macaulay—an issue on which Collins sharply disagreed with Saintsbury. More seriously, Saintsbury had tabulated thirty-four dates incorrectly and got at least four major historical facts wrong; the book, moreover, was generally rambling and incoherent: 'Whether Professor Saintsbury's duties extend to instructing the ingenuous youth of Scotland in the principles of good taste, criticism, and composition, and to training them in habits of accuracy and thoroughness, we do not know; if they do, the ingenuous youth of Scotland will probably find it necessary to supplement that instruction.' Once again, Collins' conscientious anger breaking out into sarcastic gibes spoilt his better case.

Such frenzied assaults on accuracy, however, did produce a certain self-consciousness in the writers concerned. Gosse, for example, in the preface to his *History of Eighteenth Century Literature* (1889) wrote 'Among my thousands of dates, though I have carefully revised them, some must be wrong. Any corrections of fact will be very gratefully received by myself or the publishers.'[13] Saintsbury, too, made some effort to move in the same direction. In the preface to his *Short History of English Literature* (1898), he appealed for generosity in the matter: 'None but a charlatan will pretend that he has himself written, and none but a very unreasonable person will expect any one else to write, a history of the kind free from blunders.'[14] Collins might have been unreasonable in this way but at least people were taking some notice.

Saintsbury's appeal for tolerance fell on deaf ears where Collins was concerned and the *Short History of English Literature* was subjected to the familiar scrutiny.[15] After the sarcastic heading ('A Scotch Professor on English Literature') and another sarcastic comment on Saintsbury's professorial role, Collins then proceeded to list the book's journalistic failings. For example:

> On page 2 the Professor tells us that there is no rhyme in Anglo-Saxon poetry; on page 18 we find him giving an account of the rhyming poem in the *Exeter Book*.

> On page 360 we are told that Phineas Fletcher's *Piscatory Eclogues*, which are, of course, confounded with his *Sicelides*, are a masque.

> On page 358, Brutus, the legendary founder of Britain, is actually described as the son of Aeneas. (He was of course the great-grandson.)

> Akenside's stilted and frigid *Odes* 'fall not so far short of Collins' '. We wonder what Mr Saintsbury's criterion of poetry can be. But we forget, with what criterion he has furnished us. On page 732, speaking of 'a story about a hearer who knew no English, but knew Tennyson to be a poet by the hearing', he adds that 'the story is probable and valuable, or rather invaluable, for it points to the best if not the only criterion of poetry.' And this is a critic.

In addition to matters of fact, there were clearly matters of taste and temperament at odds here: Collins was obviously infuriated not merely by Saintsbury's slipshod way with facts but also by his general woolliness which contrasted sharply with his own clean-cut assertiveness. As an example of Saintsbury's style he quotes the following:

> What the *Voyage and Travaile* really is, is this—it is, so far as we know, and even beyond our knowledge in all probability and likelihood, the first considerable example of prose in English dealing neither with the beaten track of theology and philosophy, nor with the, even in the Middle Ages, restricted field of history and home topography, but expatiating freely on unguarded plains and

on untrodden hills, sometimes dropping into actual prose romance and always treating its subject as the poets had treated theirs in *Brut* and *Morte d'Arthur*, in *Troy-Book* and *Alexandreid*, as a mere canvas on which to embroider flowers of fancy.[16]

This kind of convoluted rambling was just as detestable as Symonds' gush and Swinburne's rant. Saintsbury to his credit—unlike Symonds, Gosse and Swinburne—showed no lasting resentment at this criticism and always spoke reasonably of Collins.[17]

3

Collins hammered away at his favourite themes through the 1890s, upholding what he saw as true critical and scholarly standards and making enemies of the professors, the log-rollers and the aesthetes. All this time of course he was building up his image as the carping louse on the locks of literature. Not that this bothered Collins overmuch since he was convinced of his mission to shake up the literary world; so much so, in fact, that in 1901 he brought together several of his *Saturday* articles together with a few other pieces in a volume called *Ephemera Critica*. The aim was to present a forceful review of the general state of literary culture from the world of writing and publishing to the universities.

The book opens with an essay entitled 'The Present Functions of Criticism'; another tribute to Arnold of course but with none of Arnold's urbanity. The literary world as pictured by Collins was in a sorry state; what with literary cliques and factions, unscrupulous publishers and a superabundance of second-rate literature, genuine authors and critics had a hard time of it getting themselves published and heard. Even worse, true, proper and decent critical standards had disappeared in a welter of something called 'criticism' but in reality nothing more than subjective effusion, 'dithyramb' and 'rhetoric':

> Without standards, without touchstones, without knowledge, it appears to be the one calling for which no equipment and no training are needed ... Such canons as these 'critics' have are the mysterious and somewhat perplexing evolutions of their own inner consciousness, or derived, not from the study of classical writers in English or in any other language, of all of whom they are probably

profoundly ignorant, but from a current acquaintance with the writings of contemporaries, who are, in intelligence and performance a little in advance of themselves.[18]

Apart from a brief mention of Richard Le Gallienne, Collins does not name names here, but is obviously including anyone tainted by the current aesthetic and impressionistic mode—that is, the whole tribe of Swinburnian tasters—the lesser Zimris of criticism.[19] Against these, serious critics—Dean Church, Mark Pattison, Leslie Stephen and Frederic Harrison[20]—found it difficult to get a hearing. In attacking the modish literary world Collins, of course, was merely saying of the 1890s what had already been said by Mill, Carlyle and Arnold of earlier decades.

But unlike his predecessors, Collins also laid a great part of the blame for the present state of literary culture on the universities, and directly or indirectly a good many chapters of *Ephemera Critica* take up, yet again, the favourite Collinsian theme of the universities' neglect of literature and literary studies. It might have been thought that Collins had said all that could be said on this issue, but in fact *Ephemera Critica* was published in close connexion with another of his Oxford campaigns. For some years Collins had been pondering the possibility of getting Oxford to set up a scholarship for the comparative study of English and classical literature. Jowett had cautiously backed this idea in February 1888,[21] and now in 1901 Collins set in motion an actual proposal by gaining the support of John Passmore Edwards, a well-known philanthropist. Edwards showed some interest in the scheme and Collins with his usual alacrity and enthusiasm set about providing favourable testimonies from influential Oxford men. After some setbacks, Edwards finally agreed to endow a scholarship worth £45 p.a. and tenable for three years. This proposal was gladly accepted at Oxford and in April 1901 Collins was congratulated on his successful work in the matter.[22] A single scholarship was perhaps little to show for fifteen years effort, but at least it was a tangible result.

The scholarship scheme owed much to *Ephemera Critica* for its success; the *Oxford Magazine* for example linked it directly with the book.[23] Both the scholarship and the book also helped to focus attention on the Oxford English School once again. Since 1894, in fact, the School had existed in a state of almost permanent crisis; the language side was of course reasonably well provided for but the literary side depended mainly on the energy of a single lecturer—Ernest de Selincourt. Not surprisingly, the School attracted very few students: in four years there were only sixteen male candidates in the final examinations to forty-eight females and the rumour went around that the School existed only for the 'ladies and the Greekless'.[24] This situation was reviewed by the *Oxford Magazine* in 1901, and Collins' strictures were tardily recalled:

> There is a great deal of wholesome truth in the criticism which Mr Churton Collins has advanced from time to time, though his readers may complain that his language is wanting in moderation . . . No one will regret that the School of English Literature has been spared the fate of becoming 'a soft option'; but surely this result might be secured without insisting unduly upon the study of Gothic and the text of Beowulf. Some examiners in the School, and some teachers as well, appear to forget that there is any English literature later than the time of Chaucer. No wonder that the Greats man, who takes a fifth year's residence, leaves 'English Literature' to the Ladies' Colleges.[25]

This situation was unlikely to improve until a Professor of English Literature could be appointed.

Ephemera Critica, then, paid off in terms of its impact on the situation at Oxford, but since the bulk of the book consisted of the hard-hitting reviews Collins had been writing over the years, its cultural and educational message tended to be obscured. The reviews themselves as would be expected, received the most attention. The general reaction to the book was expressed by the *Academy*:

> it is far from our intention to belittle the service Mr Collins has rendered to literature in his efforts to introduce more of the scientific spirit and a riper scholarship into criticism. But we suggest that his pin-pricks might have been less frequent and less vicious.[26]

Collins, it was wearily implied, would never learn how to make his valuable points without overstepping the bounds of good taste and fair criticism. 'Criticism', the *Academy* reviewer remarked, 'should be sympathetic as well as destructive.' Collins might be right when he saw particular authors and critics as careless, extravagant and wilful; right too when he accused them of forming cliques 'for the purpose of mutual puffery',[27] but he could surely have made his points against them without resorting to a barrage of terms like 'nonsense', 'ludicrous', 'disgusting', 'scandalous', 'absurd', and so on, and without inventing sarcastic terms like 'Gossing' for his index. Collins seemed to be becoming paranoid in his view of literary corruption and decadence and increasingly aggressive in his tone as the years passed. Arthur Symons remarked of the book: 'Its aim is almost wholly polemical, it is meant to hit, not to please; nearly every essay is a brick thrown at somebody with great energy and a formidable sense of duty.'[28] What might be acceptable language in private literary conversations, or even in the pages of the *Pall Mall Gazette* or the *Saturday Review*, was highly offensive and off-putting when confronted at large in a book of nearly four hundred pages.

4

As it happened, though, Collins took very little interest in the reception of *Ephemera Critica*—he was suffering at the time from the worst of his periodic bouts of acute depression. On 23 January 1901, he wrote in his notebook: 'It would be impossible for a human being to be more depressed than I am, not a ray of hope is discernible, the future and its work is shuddering horror to me to contemplate.'[29] This state of total despair lasted on and off for several months and even the success of *Ephemera Critica* and the Passmore Edwards scholarship gave him no pleasure or relief. He wrote to his brother about his state of mind in April:

> For the last six months or more I have had an awful time—a sheath of melancholia has got hold of me, draining my whole life of all joy and 'lilt' and elasticity: my sufferings have been quite awful and God knows how I have managed to get through my work, but I have got through it, through every iota of it, nor lost one guinea. If it hadn't been for my dear ones here at home I couldn't possibly have struggled against it ... I fancy this horrible thing must be hereditary—do you know whether any ancestor suffered in this way, I fancy our father did.[30]

The doctors could find nothing physically wrong with him and recommended rest, a change of scene and bathing, all of which brought about some improvement, though Collins was well aware that the depression could return at any time:

> The strange thing is that there has been no reason at all for the change nor has it been aided by any means in my power. The one thing which I have certainly found to be beneficial was a cold plunge in the morning ... This attack has shown me that what I have been suffering from was a disease as much out of my power to prevent or cure as any other physical disease could be.[31]

Intensive bouts of lecturing and writing sometimes allowed Collins to forget his problems, but his tendency to morbid introspection was always lurking under the surface of his energetic bustle.

Despite his constant battle against depression, Collins felt confident enough in the aftermath of *Ephemera Critica* and the Passmore Edwards scholarship to make one further application for an Oxford Chair. Earle, the Professor of Anglo-Saxon, died in 1903 and by the provisions made nine years earlier, the Chairs of Anglo-Saxon and English were combined under Napier, thus allowing the University to set up a Chair of English Literature in its own right. Collins could justifiably feel that he had some claim on this Chair and lost no time in applying for it when it was advertised early in 1904. In his letter of application,[32] he once again stressed his wide experience as a lecturer in English literature and pointed out that nearly all his energies had gone into 'anonymous miscellaneous literature' and into his Extension work. He therefore hoped that the Oxford post would allow him time to make 'more solid contributions to literary history and criticism than I have as yet had the opportunity of making'.

By 1904, of course, Collins was able to offer much greater testimonial support than in his first application for an Oxford chair twenty years earlier. In his first application he offered four testimonials; in the second twenty-six, most of them gathered together in the intervening years as he began to look for university posts. Among those who provided support for Collins were Henry Morley, Jowett, John Rhys (Professor of Celtic at Oxford), W. J. Courthope, Edward Dowden, J. W. Hales and Andrew Lang. The rest comprised a range of Professors (R. C. Jebb of Cambridge, T.

R. Lounsbury of Yale), literary scholars (F. J. Furnivall, Henry Craik, Leslie Stephen), and a number of Oxford acquaintances and former students. The general feeling was that Collins deserved the post. Rhys for example, who had been 'profoundly impressed' by Collins' demonstration of the link between English literature and Classics, spoke of the appropriateness of having Collins in a university 'which is nothing if not devoted to Latin and Greek'. Both Courthope and Dowden acknowledged a debt to his literary writings and Dowden added a note on his abilities: 'Few living writers have been more energetic in research in the field of English literature; few have been more accurate, clear and vigorous in statement.' Andrew Lang, who was unenthusiastic about Extension work said 'it is a grief to me that his time has been so much occupied with teaching classes when he might have been teaching all of us in books'.

Many of Collins' supporters also spoke of his attractive personal qualities; of his charm, amiability, enthusiasm and generosity—qualities not readily apparent to readers of his reviews. All in all Collins was a strong candidate for the post. He was an excellent teacher and a sound scholar who might do even more impressive work given more time to research. He had established himself as a leading spokesman on the subject of literary education and was respected by writers and teachers the world over. If anyone could revive the fortunes of the Oxford English School, and possibly of Classics too, Collins was the man. As he must have known himself, though, Collins was totally unacceptable to Oxford, or at least to official bodies at Oxford. Whatever his abilities as a teacher and scholar, he had spent far too many years abusing Oxford attitudes, degree structures and syllabuses, to be rewarded with a chair. Besides, with his well-publicized convictions about the need for radical upheavals in the universities, who knew what havoc he might cause in sedate Oxford circles if he was given a professorship.

The post was offered instead to—from Oxford's point of view—a much more readily appealing figure, Walter Raleigh, who although younger than Collins had already held chairs at Liverpool and Glasgow. Raleigh had published safe, readable books on *The English Novel* (1894), *Milton* (1899) and *Wordsworth* (1903), and a more daring and flashy one called *Style* (1897), which Collins had reviewed for the *Saturday*, calling it 'the most intolerable piece of literary coxcombry which it has ever been our irritating ill-fortune to meet with'.[33] Raleigh's appointment at Oxford was engineered by his supporters there, including T. H. Warren, W. P. Ker and probably A. C. Bradley.[34] T. H. Warren in fact might have been justifiably accused of some double-dealing in the matter: he was an old friend of Collins, the friendship dating from their student days at Balliol, he had encouraged Collins in his various Oxford enterprises, including the Passmore Edwards scholarship scheme, and also wrote a flattering testimonial for him in support of his Oxford application. Had Collins known about this manoeuvring, he would have felt once again that he was being excluded from positions he deserved by cliqueish conspiracies. On the other hand, Oxford could argue that he was naive to believe that his application would ever be taken seriously.

Ironically, Raleigh's appointment to the Chair at Oxford helped Collins himself to a university post. Raleigh's move to Oxford left the Glasgow Chair vacant; his successor there was W. Macneile Dixon, who had been Professor of English at Birmingham University. Shortly after his Oxford disappointment, Collins applied for the Birmingham Chair and this time, no doubt to his amazement, was successful. The Birmingham post was obviously less attractive than the Oxford one, but it did at least give him some official academic recognition and status, and since Birmingham was not too far from London it allowed him to keep in touch with his Extension and other interests.

NOTES

1   L. C. Collins, op. cit., pp. 303–04.

2   Frank Harris, *Latest Contemporary Portraits*, 1927, p. 313.

3   *Saturday Review*, 24 November 1894, pp. 562–63; 1 December 1894, pp. 602–03; 8 December 1894, pp. 623–24.

4   See *Some Reminiscences of William Michael Rossetti*, 2 vols., 1906, II, 385–86.

5   *Saturday Review*, 26 October 1895, pp. 550–51.

6   L. C. Collins, op. cit., p. 158.

7   For Saintsbury see *George Saintsbury: Essays and Papers*, 1945, which

contains a biographical memoir by A. Blyth Webster and other personal portraits; and Wellek, op. cit., IV, 416–28.

8   See, for example, *The Letters of Sir Walter Raleigh*, ed. Lady Raleigh, 2 vols., 1926, I, 186. L. C. Collins, however, is silent on the matter.

9   *Saturday Review*, 30 November 1895, pp. 725–26.

10 Ibid., p. 726.

11 Ibid., 18 January 1896, pp. 67–68.

12 Ibid., 25 April 1896, pp. 423–25.

13 Edmund Gosse, *A History of Eighteenth Century Literature*, 1889, p. viii.

14 George Saintsbury, *A Short History of English Literature*, 1898, p. vi.

15 *Saturday Review*, 3 December 1898, pp. 738–39.

16 Ibid., p. 739.

17 *George Saintsbury: Essays and Papers*, p. 15.

18 J. C. Collins, *Ephemera Critica*, pp. 26–27.

19 See above, p. 57.

20 *Ephemera Critica*, p. 35.

21 Jowett to Collins, letter dated 6 February 1888. Balliol College Library.

22 L. C. Collins, op. cit., p. 171.

23 Ibid., p. 171.

24 C. Oman, *Memories of Victorian Oxford*, 1941, p. 239.

25 *Oxford Magazine*, 29 May 1901, p. 375.

26 *Academy*, 9 March 1901, p. 203.

27 *Ephemera Critica*, p. 20.

28 *Fortnightly Review*, LXXV, June 1901, p. 1004.

29 L. C. Collins, op. cit., p. 235.

30 Ibid., pp. 237–38.

31 Ibid., p. 241.

32 Collins' testimonials and application for the Oxford Chair of English Literature are in the Bodleian Library.

33 *Saturday Review*, 20 November 1897, p. 536.

34 Palmer, op. cit., p. 122.

CHAPTER EIGHT

THE ENGLISH PROFESSOR

Collins' first, understandably cautious, approaches to Birmingham University were made through Dixon himself. Early in October 1904 he wrote to Dixon, saying that he was interested in the post and asking if he had Dixon's 'approbation'. Collins offered to send on his Oxford testimonials but wanted to keep his application private. He told Dixon he was very anxious to avoid the humiliation of a public rejection and was clearly sensitive about his previous failures.[1]

The other candidates were F. S. Boas, G. C. Macaulay, and Professors Litterdale and Walker of Cardiff and Lampeter. An interesting correspondence was soon in progress about these candidates between H. G. Fiedler, Dean of the Faculty of Arts at Birmingham and Edward Dowden of Trinity College Dublin, one of Collins' referees for the Oxford post. Dowden said of Collins 'he is always learned, vigorous, trenchant, combative, a writer of strong views & pronounced opinions, & in no degree tamed by his fifty-six years—I mean in the spirit with which he drives home his opinions.' Dowden also made comments on the other candidates and spoke highly of Litterdale and Boas.[2]

In the event, Collins' combination of vigour and learning and well-known teaching ability was preferred and Dixon's support was probably the deciding factor. On 15 December, the day the appointment was made, he was reported in *The Times* as saying of Collins: 'He would bring the University real distinction, great experience as a teacher, unusual lecturing power, and the ripest and most mature scholarship. His recent work is as virile and brilliant as anything he has done. I should consider you most fortunate if you get him.'[3] Oliver Lodge, Principal of Birmingham University, supported this view when he told a Governors' Meeting in February 1905 that they had been very 'fortunate in obtaining a world-known scholar like Professor Churton Collins'.[4]

A private tribute was also paid by Henry Sweet, one of Collins' old philological opponents; in a letter to Fiedler soon after the appointment he wrote 'Birmingham has done well in appointing C. Collins: he is quite genuine. He ought to have been a professor at Oxford long ago.'[5]

Birmingham University, which received its charter in 1900, had a distinctive utilitarian bias in its early days. Its real history began in 1880 with the opening of the Mason Science College. The Science College was mainly intended to further scientific studies in relation to local industry, and while liberal subjects were never entirely excluded, its founder, Sir Josiah Mason, a self-made industrialist, had wanted to discourage 'mere literary instruction and education'. The College opened with four chairs: Mathematics, Physics, Chemistry and Biology, and a year later a gesture towards liberal education was made with the setting up of chairs in Classics and English.[6] By 1899, however, with further chairs in the sciences and in Metallurgy, Engineering and Brewing, the College was strongly weighted against the Arts subjects.

The University at the outset, then, seemed to have little interest in the Humanities, and indeed in his first report the Principal referred to 'an unfortunate impression abroad that Birmingham either does not possess or does not encourage a Faculty of Arts'.[7] Collins' appointment to the Chair of English was obviously part of a move to strengthen the Arts side in the University and in cooperation with the Professor of Classics, E. A. Sonnenschein, he was soon making proposals to bring literary studies into more prominence.

The requirements for the Arts degree at Birmingham were similar to those for the London B.A. which they superseded; English was one of five subjects which could be taken in the final examinations—three Principal subjects and two Subsidiary (from 1903–04, two Principal subjects and one Subsidiary subject could be taken).[8] For the M.A. a further year's study was required in one or two subjects. Once installed at Birmingham, Collins soon began to make changes in the English courses, adding writers who might be studied with special attention to the classical influence and increasing the number of critics on each course.[9] These changes precisely reflected the ideas he had been putting forward since the 1880s, and by adding critics like Aristotle, Longinus,

Lessing, Schiller and Saint-Beuve to the syllabus he was remedying what he saw as scandalous defects in the Oxford English School.

A more surprising aspect of Collins' syllabus reforms at Birmingham is the attention he gave to early literature. Unlike Dixon he began the course with the 'origins' of the subject and throughout laid stress on Middle English, making Anglo-Saxon compulsory for the M.A. The explanation is either that he wanted to answer his critics who had earlier accused him of mindless hostility to early literature (when it came to designing an English syllabus he could be as well-balanced as anybody!), or that, by this time, after his failure to get the chair at University College London in 1889 through his ignorance of Anglo-Saxon, he had developed a stronger interest in the subject. In any case, as early as 1897 he was recommending a study of the elements of Anglo-Saxon in the middle stages of secondary schooling,[10] and it seems likely that even by this stage he was beginning to consider early literature a matter for serious study, even if it had much less attraction for him than Classics. There is no evidence that Collins ever became proficient in Anglo-Saxon (much of the teaching of it at Birmingham was done by the German Department) but early literature seems to have aroused his speculations. After his death in some of his unpublished lecture notes was found the question: 'Was the author of Beowulf acquainted with the Iliad?'[11] The question remained unanswered but one can see Collins eagerly adding to his ever-enlarging list of possible influences and connexions. This probably explains the continuance of *Beowulf* on the Birmingham English course, despite his earlier contempt for it.

This aside, Collins remained convinced to the end that the main concern of the English literature course was the great literary tradition from the time of Chaucer onwards. The English classics, of course, were to be studied in their relation to classical and European influences, and Collins was fortunate here in having a strong ally in E. A. Sonnenschein, the Professor of Classics. Sonnenschein's literary interests were very similar to Collins' and it is almost certain that he had some say in his appointment to the Chair of English. For Sonnenschein, as for Collins, the study of literature was essentially the study of the great minds of the past, and at the Summer Extension Meeting at Oxford in 1892, he had argued that 'the truly literary aspect of literary subjects is far too much neglected. We treat the classics as subjects for the grammatical microscope or the historical telescope, and forget that Homer and Virgil, Goethe and Molière are great poets.'[12] Since Collins was also lecturing at Oxford at this time, it is probable that he met Sonnenschein then. In any case their similarity of literary outlook led to a correspondence later.

In April 1901, Sonnenschein wrote to Collins asking for advice about the 'literary study of Greek and Latin'. He was hoping, he said, to 'shift the centre of gravity of the teaching' in Classics at Birmingham from language to literature, and wondered if Collins could suggest good translations which would introduce students to a wider field of literature. Sonnenschein also mentioned that Dixon favoured the scheme and said that he hoped for a selection of texts which might be of 'most service to the student of English literature'.[13] Collins of course was flattered to be approached in this way and sent on a list of translations he had found useful in his Extension classes and also a list of English writers, Milton, Shelley, Arnold, Dryden, Pope, Johnson, Gray and Tennyson, who could be most profitably studied in relation to classical authors.[14] Further correspondence followed and there can be no doubt that Sonnenschein's presence at Birmingham was an important factor in Collins' later application there.

Collins' most important contribution to the development of English studies at Birmingham was the setting up of a School of English Literature in 1907–08 (a School of Classics was set up in the same session). This School was a sensibly modified version of the School of Literature he had been clamouring for during the previous twenty years, offering a three year course leading to the M.A. degree as an alternative to the existing scheme. In the new School students were able to study one Principal subject English (instead of two in the other scheme) together with a Subsidiary subject Latin and one additional subject studied for two years, Greek or Italian or French or German. The final examination in English comprised papers on the History of English literature, set books, literary theory, Anglo-Saxon and Middle English, the influence of Latin and other literatures on English (two papers), English history, Philosophy.[15]

It was here that Collins was able to realize his ambition to develop comparative literary studies to some degree, and along with questions on English authors and English history, students were asked to discuss such things as:

> Estimate the nature and extent of Spenser's indebtedness to Plato and Aristotle.
>
> Trace the influence of Greek ideas in the poetry of Shelley.
>
> How far would it be true to say that the history of English literature in its mature expression is little more than the history of the modification of Celtic and Teutonic elements by classical influence?[16]

These of course were testing questions but readers of Chapter 5 of Collins' *The Study of English Literature* would have had a fair idea of the kind of answers he expected. Even earlier he was asking his Extension students to consider similar issues and now the Birmingham English courses simply gave formal shape to his life-long concern with comparative literary studies. Phrases like 'in its mature expression' exposed an in-built bias to the course, but Collins could have argued that all courses are slanted in one way or another.

Meanwhile Collins was working in co-operation with Sonnenschein to bring the two Schools of English and Classics closer together. A new course on the 'Literature of Greece in translations' was added to the list of Subsidiary subjects for the B.A. in 1908 and shortly afterwards this subject together with Ancient History could also be offered as a Principal subject by those taking Latin at Principal level. Writing of this 'experiment' in September 1908, Sonnenschein said 'By co-operation between the Professors of English and Classics it has been arranged that the courses of reading in English Literature and in Latin and Greek shall illustrate one another ... Thus treated, Classics and English Literature form parts of an organised whole, and the studies gain greatly in vitality.'[17] What certain Oxford classicists had been arguing for back in the 1880s was now being put into practice not at Oxford but at Birmingham, and the University whose Arts Faculty had been in some doubt was now showing Oxford how literary studies should be organized.

Collins' sudden death in 1908 of course put an end to his educational experiments, but during the three and a half years he was at Birmingham he clearly revitalized the English Department there in more than one way. During his time as Professor the number of students taking English nearly doubled, an Essay Club and a Shakespeare Society were founded, and through his regular interpretative recitals—lectures-cum-readings—he captivated large audiences of students and townsfolk.[18] Collins of course continued to work at a hectic pace throughout this time, and until the arrival of Michael Macmillan to assist him in the 1906–07 session, virtually ran the whole English course singlehanded. Until the end of 1907 he also continued with a good deal of Extension teaching, travelling between Birmingham and London every week on a regular basis: a record of a typical week's work in October 1906, for example, shows him lecturing at the University, at Tamworth and Wolverhampton, and at several different venues in London on thirteen different subjects between Monday and Saturday.[19]

2

During his last years, Collins also found time for research and writing between his teaching and syllabus reorganizing. Between 1904 and 1908 he published *Studies in Shakespeare* (1904), *Studies in Poetry and Criticism* (1905) and *Voltaire, Montesquieu and Rousseau in England* (1908). Two more books prepared just before his death appeared afterwards: his *Greek Influence on English Poetry* (1910) and *Posthumous Essays* (1912). He also published what turned out to be a shoddily prepared edition of the *Plays and Poems of Robert Greene* (1905), which was given Collinsian treatment by W. W. Greg in the *Modern Language Review*.[20] All these books either rework or extend Collins' previous interests and the Birmingham post clearly did not give the time he had hoped for to break new ground. But *Studies in Shakespeare* and *Studies in Poetry and Criticism* are certainly worth glancing at here.

When it came to Shakespeare, Collins was as adulatory as any late Victorian critic: he taught him to countless Extension classes over the years and worried over the various Shakespearean questions which exercised the minds of contemporary scholars and critics. The titles of some of the chapters of *Studies in Shakespeare* show his typical preoccupations with this subject: 'Shakespeare as a classical scholar'; 'Sophocles and Shakespeare as Theological and Ethical Teachers'; 'Was Shakespeare a lawyer?'; 'The Bacon-Shakespeare mania'. On the last two matters here Collins was creditably level-headed and argued convincing cases in the name of reason and commonsense: Shakespeare was certainly well-versed in legal matters and terminology and may well have worked in an attorney's office at some stage, but the evidence is not conclusive; as for the Bacon–Shakespeare issue, Collins found this to be totally preposterous; 'It is not so much by its absurdity as by the absence of everything which could give colour to that absurdity, that the Bacon–Shakespeare myth holds a unique place among literary follies.'[21] On the first issue, however, 'Shakespeare as a classical scholar', Collins' clearheadedness gave way to wishful thinking; where the classical influence was at issue he was always carried away by his obsessive need to drag everyone into it.

The question of Shakespeare's knowledge of the Classics had already been dealt with by Victorian scholars and critics, including the American critic, James Russell Lowell, in *Among My Books* (1898). All of these had argued the reasonable case that Shakespeare knew Latin well and might well have had access to Greek drama through Latin translations. Collins, however, wished to go further:

> what merit my paper may have lies in the fact that it is very much fuller than anything which so far as my knowledge goes, has yet appeared on the subject; that it suggests and marshals many new arguments in favour of the extended hypothesis that the poet was not merely a fair Latin scholar, but that his knowledge of the classics both of Greece and Rome was remarkably extensive; and that it supports these arguments with illustrations more numerous than can be found elsewhere.[22]

Following the procedures he adopted earlier in his study of Tennyson, Collins set out to show that, if Shakespeare knew no Greek, his competence in Latin allowed him to acquire a much greater knowledge of the Greek classics through Latin versions than anyone had yet suspected.

As with the Tennyson volume, the main impression left by 'Shakespeare as a classical scholar' is one of amazement at Collins' vast classical reading and detailed knowledge of Shakespeare; the essay is a huge mosaic of quotations and poetic parallels drawn from every quarter of Shakespeare and the Greek and Roman poets. Collins to begin with is reasonably cautious about the question of direct imitations: 'In dealing with Shakespeare's probable obligations to the Greek dramatists, we have obviously to be on our guard against three things'; these three things are parallel 'commonplaces', 'likely to be mere coincidences'; similarities of expression ('And yet such similarities as the following are very remarkable'—thirty or forty examples follow); and similarities of sentiment 'under similar circumstances'.[23] None of these, says Collins, can be taken as evidence of any direct borrowing by Shakespeare from the Greeks; and yet the sheer volume of parallels clearly fascinates him to such an extent that he is soon moving from speculation to conviction. For example:

> Not less remarkable are parallels in idioms and in peculiarities of diction and rhythm which might be attributed partly to the influence of our classical drama, partly to the unfixed and experimental methods of composition characteristic of the Elizabethan poets, and partly to Shakespeare's own boundless fertility and plasticity of expression, but which might also have originated from direct imitation.[24]

Collins of course could not be absolutely sure of his case for direct borrowing (Tennyson was a much surer case), but he obviously felt that it would be a pity if Shakespeare had not imitated the Greeks. He thus quickly moves into something like assertion: 'Nothing could be more purely Greek than the dialogue in monostichs in *Richard III*'; 'How purely classical, with the note of Euripides, is the dialogue between Iris and Ceres in the fourth act of the *Tempest*'; 'It is not likely that Shakespeare could read Greek with facility, but if he possessed enough of it to follow the original Latin version, as he probably did, he would not only be able to enrich his diction with its idioms and phraseology but would acquire that *timbre* in style of which I have given illustrations.'[25] The remainder of the essay goes into details regarding other parallels between Shakespeare and the Greeks—questions of dramatic structure, irony, thought, metaphysics and morality— and concludes by summarizing the evidence: Shakespeare could read Latin; the Greek dramatists were available to him in Latin versions; it is highly probable that he read those versions and that the characteristics of his own work which are different from those of his contemporary dramatists are probably—Collins implies 'certainly'—'attributable to the influence of those dramatists'.[26]

Collins' essay was an impressive performance, demonstrating his marvellous powers of recall, but it was scarcely a disinterested one. In the first place he tended to assume what he was setting out to prove, and secondly his case for Shakespeare's indebtedness to the classics of Greece and Rome was all too obviously related to his campaign for linking English and Classics. Subsequent investigations of the subject show that Collins overstated his case for the Greek influence on Shakespeare and that most of what can be called the 'Greek outlook' in his plays came from his reading of Plutarch rather than from his knowledge of the Greek dramatists.[27]

Collins' essay on 'Sophocles and Shakespeare as Theological and Ethical Teachers' is a more plausible Arnoldian piece, suggesting not the influence of Sophocles on Shakespeare but their essential kinship as great moralists and teachers (Arnold, however, is taken to task by Collins for not taking Shakespeare sufficiently seriously in this way). Once again Collins draws exhaustive parallels between Sophocles and Shakespeare as philosophers, though he argues that Sophocles is fundamentally more religious than Shakespeare. The essay is mainly of interest here for the light it throws on Collins' own poetic-cum-religious faith—for example:

> We have long begun to feel more and more that the message which God sent by the Evangelists, save only in the record of the perfect life, has been miserably marred and blurred in the telling. But how sun-clear, how consistent with themselves and with each other, how corresponsive and mutually corroborative are the messages which have come to us through His other evangelists. The authors of the Psalms, the Hebrew Prophets, Homer, Pindar, Aeschylus, Sophocles, Virgil, Dante, Spenser, Shakespeare, Milton, Goethe, Wordsworth, Shelley, and we may add, whether *longo intervallo* or not Posterity will decide, Tennyson and Browning. Have they not pierced through different time-veils to the same eternal truths and preached, each in his own manner and with his own symbols, the same authentic gospel? The more men come to distinguish between what is local and what is universal, between what is accidental and what is essential, the more will they come to realize that as ethical truth is the immediate test of theological truth, so poetical truth is the final test of both.[28]

Inheriting most of his important beliefs and ideas from Carlyle
and Arnold, Collins eagerly turns Sophocles and Shakespeare—
with a total disregard for history—into the great teachers of
humanity. Both Sophocles and Shakespeare were admired, not
because they offered clear answers to the basic problems of human
life—'To both poets there was much in life and in the ways of God
with men which presented insoluble problems'—but because they
deliberately confronted these problems in the heart of their work.
In this way, Collins finds the supposed parallels between the two
poets less important than the fact of their common search for a
philosophy of life; consequently they can be seen as particularly
relevant to an age experiencing a general loss of direction. Not
least of all, of course, their seriousness of purpose, together with
their demonstrable powers as dramatists, made them excellent
subjects for literary study. Moreover, by linking the two poets
together, Collins was also making out a case for Shakespeare
which would enhance his place in the academic curriculum
alongside the very best of the Classical poets.

Collins' debt to Arnold can also be seen in *Studies in Poetry and
Criticism*, where a fundamental note of optimism is sounded despite
the prevailing gloom:

> Literature generally will degenerate, as it has degenerated, into
> little more than a means of affording recreation and amusement to
> those whose serious interests and occupations are elsewhere; and
> poetry will cease to appeal, or will share, as it now shares, in this
> degradation. But man's finer and nobler energies can only be
> depressed, they can never be extinguished or even lose their vitality.
> Unerring and inevitable as the law of gravitation in the physical, is
> the law of reaction in the spiritual world. Materialism—and let us
> understand the word in its most comprehensive sense—has still a
> long course to run, of that we may be sure. But all that poetry
> represents and vindicates can never fail at last to assert itself.[29]

Such unity as this book has is provided by Collins' search for
particular literary standards and values, culminating in a chapter
which paraphrases Arnold's views more or less explicitly. Conscious of the fact that he might well be accused of looking for
standards of poetic greatness only in the past, Collins spends
several chapters of this volume evaluating modern poetry. A long
chapter on 'Poetry and Poets of America' singles out Bryant,

Emerson and Lowell for special praise, while Whitman is demoted
from the high place given him by Symonds ('It is pitiable to see a
critic like Addington Symonds exalting Whitman into a bard and
prophet').[30] In England, after Tennyson, Browning and Swinburne, Collins finds William Watson and Gerald Massey to be the
most interesting modern poets.

Massey is the main surprise of the *Studies in Poetry and Criticism*
volume since he was so decidedly minor a poet that his name rarely
appears in the standard histories of literature. Poetic ability
apart, his main interest for Collins was a type of struggling
genius—the sort of writer Collins was always immediately
attracted to. Born into poverty and obscurity in the early nineteenth century (his father was 'a canal boatman of the ordinary
type, supporting on ten shillings a week, in a wretched hovel, a
numerous family'),[31] Massey by a laborious self-education and
superhuman effort succeeded in producing poetry of sufficient
quality to attract the attention of Landor, who hailed him as a
new Keats. Massey wrote 'revolutionary lyrics' about social and
political injustice, and was inspired by the Chartist Movement and
later by the Crimean war to produce poems full of beauty,
suffering and pathos. According to Collins he also showed much
originality and power; something Collins was happy to pay a late
tribute to in his essay. But plainly enough his main interest was as a
resilient genius—an inglorious Milton who refused to stay mute:
'His career affords one of the most striking examples on record of
the power of genius to assert itself under conditions as unfavour-
able and malign as ever contributed to thwart and depress it.'[32]
Collins wisely refrained from trying to assess Massey's 'relative
position among the poets of the Victorian era' but he clearly saw
him as someone worth attention in an age of triflers and aesthetes.
Massey had character which gave 'an attractiveness to his poetry
quite irrespective of its merits as mere poetry, just as in human
features there is often a beauty and a charm which is simply the
reflection of moral character'.[33]

Collins' essay on William Watson had a similar personal slant to
it. Collins was on friendly terms with Watson, and apart from
liking his poetry up to a point, had at least one thing in common
with him: Watson's father, like Collins' uncle, was a worldly
businessman, who tried to discourage his son's interest in literature

but, like Collins, Watson had persisted in his literary interests and had become a successful poet.[34] Collins admired the 'classical quality' in Watson's verse, which of course stood in contrast to the flamboyance and excess of much poetry of the 1890s, and felt that it had some 'elements of permanence'. Watson, however, like Arnold and Gray, was living in an age of 'decadence and transition' and his real gifts had never properly emerged:

> To Mr Watson's poetry with its limited and unambitious range, its comparatively few notes, its persistent threnody, its joyless agnosticism, its thin and uncertain ethic, the critics of the future will probably point, and point mournfully, as a striking example of a most rare and fine genius struggling with malign and depressive conditions.[35]

All this was said with feeling; Collins of course felt that his own message was falling on deaf ears. Collins no doubt was also disposed to think well of Watson because Watson composed an Ode to him—a poem which in itself suggests both his conventionality and enthusiasms.

TO JOHN CHURTON COLLINS

Collins, that with the elect of Greece and Rome
Dost daily in familiar converse dwell—
Have I not sat, long after bell on bell
Hath tolled the noon of night from spire and dome,
To hear you summon from their shadowy home
The laurelled ghosts obedient to your spell?
Bards from the fields of deathless asphodel,
And one with locks white as the Chian foam.

Oft be it mine, at your fireside, to meet
The phantoms that assail not, nor alarm;
The gracious lyrist of the Sabine farm,
Coming cool-thoughted from that green retreat;
Or loftier Mantuan, more divinely sweet,
Lord of the incommunicable charm.[36]

In his hierarchy of poetry, Collins chiefly admired poets who showed 'intensity', 'passion', and 'enthusiasm', so that poets like Watson and American academic poets like Longfellow, Holmes, and even Lowell, whom he admired, were rated below inspired moralists like Wordsworth and Goethe. Much as he liked classical learning and technical brilliance, he looked much more for moral fervour, nobility and uplift and sometimes found it in very odd places—if not in a William Watson then in a Stephen Phillips (his former pupil at Scoones') whose poetry Collins found equal at its most intense to Sophocles and Dante.[37] Thus while reading the American poets he admired the brilliance of Edgar Allan Poe, and talked of 'his precise and clear-cut style, so lucid, so coldly chaste, so deliberately, so exquisitely finished'. Poe, however, lacked the depth and soul Collins, like Arnold, required of the highest poetry: readers 'will marvel at its miracles of technical triumph. But they will draw no inspiration from it. It has nothing of the influential virtue of vital poetry: it carries no balm for the heart's wounds, no solace for life's cares.'[38] Sophocles, Dante and Shakespeare thus represented the highest points of great poetry, while at the other extreme came the aesthetic dabblers who 'have so abused the name of poetry, so prostituted and degraded it by light and frivolous and even by scandalous and immoral uses and associations, that, as a name, it has almost ceased to have any serious significance'.[39]

3

Though appearances were soon to prove deceptive, Collins seemed a much more relaxed and contented figure while at Birmingham University. This was certainly the impression of friends and colleagues. Walter Raleigh, who visited the University in 1905 as External Examiner in English, and who was probably not relishing the prospect of working with Collins, found him 'very humane, and curiously modest concerning universities and the way to work them'.[40] Oliver Lodge, too, noted the contrast between Collins' belligerence as a reviewer and his geniality as a colleague: 'On the senate', said Lodge, 'he was conciliatory and quiet to a marked degree.'[41] Clearly the official recognition Collins had been given as a Professor of English after years of frustrated applications helped to smooth his crusty edges. He was also delighted to hear in March 1905 that he had been awarded an Honorary D.Litt by Durham University.[42]

Collins, however, by no means lost all his fighting energies during his time as Professor at Birmingham. In addition to his academic causes, he began to turn to non-academic matters, particularly to his favourite pastime, criminology. Collins from his early days as a journalist for the *Globe* had been fascinated by crime and criminals, and L. C. Collins in Chapter 13 of his biography recounts his father's interviews with famous criminals and his interest in the grim details of particular cases, including the Jack the Ripper murders. (By coincidence, Collins was lecturing in the East End during the Autumn of 1888 when the murders took place; something that must have given a certain frisson to his talks on Milton.) Collins' interest in crime came partly from his morbid curiosity, which he indulged in visits to morgues and cemeteries but mainly from his interest in criminal psychology. As he told an interviewer in 1906,

> What fascinates me is the manifold insight into human character which you can always gain from a well-reported murder trial. It is not from any vulgar taste for horror that I have given so much time to such a subject, but from an almost morbid desire to get at facts and truth.[43]

As a remorseless investigator into all matters of fact and detail he also liked to play Sherlock Holmes and offer his own theories about various crimes. In fact he became acquainted with Conan Doyle himself in pursuit of this hobby.[44]

His greatest involvement here was with the Merstham Tunnel mystery. In September 1905, a Miss Mary Money was found dead in a railway tunnel, having first been gagged and then thrown out of the carriage she was travelling in. Since the police seemed unable to make much headway with the case Collins decided to examine all the evidence for himself and came forward with his own theories about it. He also offered strong criticism of police procedures (*National Review* December 1905 and March 1906). In the style he used on other occasions to berate the failures of the universities and the literary establishment, he now blamed the inefficiency of the police, the whole system of criminal investigation in Britain and the sensational press for publicizing key facts which alerted criminals to the progress being made. In effect he argued that the whole procedure for solving serious crime was unsatisfactory:

> The chief defects of our system of criminal investigation, defects
> mainly responsible for the appalling list of unconvicted murderers,
> are the publicity of all its proceedings, the hard conditions imposed
> on those who could assist inquiry, the inadequacy of, and fre-
> quently, the incompetence of the officials to whom at the earlier
> and most critical stages the conduct of these cases is entrusted, and
> above all, the immunity of reasonably suspected persons from
> liability to such tests and scrutiny as they are submitted to on the
> continent.[45]

The Merstham Tunnel mystery remained a mystery, though
Collins was convinced he knew who the murderer was—a 'conviction', says L. C. Collins, 'shared by Scotland Yard'.[46] Collins also
involved himself, along with Conan Doyle, in publicizing possible
cases of wrongful conviction. Doyle later wrote of him: 'He had a
great heart for any case of oppression. It made him quite frenzied
with indignation, for he had a fine sense of justice. Yet he weighed
a case well before he went into it.'[47]

All this of course was only a minor side-line of Collins' career—a
channelling of surplus energy not used up by his main campaigns
and crusades. But it is easy to see how, but for his passionate
commitment to literature, he might well have become a great
crusading editor in the cause of legal reform—someone like W. T.
Stead of the *Pall Mall Gazette*. With his obsessive concern to get at
the truth, his talent for argument and gathering influential
opinions, he would have been a great jolter of complacencies in the
legal world.

NOTES

1   Collins to Dixon, MS. letter, 1 October 1904. Birmingham Univer-
       sity Library.
2   Dowden to Fiedler, MS. letter, 15 November 1904. Birmingham
       University Library.
3   *The Times*, 15 December 1904, p. 6.
4   *Birmingham Daily Post*, 7 February 1905.
5   Sweet to Fiedler, MS. letter, 29 January 1905. Birmingham Univer-
       sity Library.
6   E. W. Vincent and P. Hinton, *The University of Birmingham*, 1947, p.
       65.

7   Cited in D. S. Brewer, 'English Studies in the University of Birmingham', *English and Germanic Studies*, III, 1949–50, p. 17.

8   *University of Birmingham Calendar*, 1900–01, p. 121, and 1903–04, pp. 261 ff.

9   *University of Birmingham Calendar*, 1905–06, pp. 296–301.

10 J. C. Collins, *The Academy*, 30 January 1897, p. 151.

11 J. C. Collins, *Greek Influence on English Poetry*, 1910, p. vii.

12 E. A. Sonnenschein, *The Educational Review*, III, November 1892, p. 26.

13 See L. C. Collins, op. cit., p. 175.

14 Ibid., pp. 176–78.

15 *University of Birmingham Calendar*, 1907–08, pp. 173 ff.

16 'School of English Literature' M.A. papers, June 1908. University of Birmingham Library.

17 E. A. Sonnenschein, 'An Experiment in University Education', *The Classical Review*, September 1908, p. 171.

18 Obituary notice of Collins in the *Mermaid*, November 1908, pp. 16–17.

19 L. C. Collins, op. cit., pp. 306–07.

20 W. W. Greg, *The Modern Language Review*, I, 1905–06, pp. 238–51.

21 J. C. Collins, *Studies in Shakespeare*, p. 333. Collins' attack on the Baconians resulted in an irate counter-attack by R. M. Theobald, one of the Baconians referred to. See R. M. Theobald, *The Ethics of Criticism: illustrated by Mr Churton Collins*, 1904. Theobald at least got an apology out of Collins: 'You are quite justified in rebuking me for the very acrimonious and contemptuous tone of my essay, but I am a man who feels very strongly on this particular subject, and therefore I have expressed myself strongly—too strongly, perhaps . . .' *The Ethics of Criticism*, p. 16.

22 *Studies in Shakespeare*, pp. v–vi.

23 Ibid., pp. 46–52.

24 Ibid., p. 59.

25 Ibid., pp. 60–63.

26 Ibid., p. 94.

27 For a discussion of this issue see J. W. Velz, *Shakespeare and the Classical Tradition*, 1968, passim.

28 *Studies in Shakespeare*, pp. 131–32. For Collins the religious element in Shakespeare was most evident in his recognition of a 'Universal Law' which controlled the physical and moral world. Ibid., pp. 152 ff. The whole essay has interesting parallels with A. C. Bradley's *Shakespearean Tragedy* also published in 1904, though it has to be said that Bradley's idea of the 'moral order' outlined in his first lecture is more

convincing than Collins'. Bradley is less concerned to be categorical about Shakespearean metaphysics than Collins. Both Collins and Bradley were influenced by T. H. Green's philosophical teachings at Balliol.

29 *Studies in Poetry and Criticism*, p. 76.

30 Ibid., p.68.

31 Ibid., p.150.

32 Ibid., p. 144.

33 Ibid., pp. 149–50.

34 L. C. Collins, op. cit., pp. 252–53.

35 *Studies in Poetry and Criticism*, p. 141.

36 Quoted in L. C. Collins, op. cit., pp. 255–56.

37 See above, p. 20. For Collins' high estimate of Phillips see *Ephemera Critica*, pp. 294 ff. Phillips, author of such poetic dramas as *Paolo and Francesca* (1899), *Herod* (1901), *Ulysses* (1904) and a non-dramatic poem *Christ in Hades* enjoyed an overblown reputation at the time as can be seen by the space given to him in F. W. Chandler's *Aspects of Modern Drama*, 1914, pp. 382–94.

38 *Studies in Poetry and Criticism*, pp. 44–45.

39 Ibid., p. 278.

40 *The Letters of Sir Walter Raleigh*, II, 279.

41 *The Times*, 3 October 1908, p. 11.

42 L. C. Collins, op. cit., p. 184.

43 *Edgbastonia*, March 1906, p. 51.

44 L. C. Collins, op. cit., pp. 203–204.

45 *Edgbastonia*, March 1906, p. 52.

46 L. C. Collins, op. cit., p. 201.

47 Ibid., p. 247.

CHAPTER NINE

THE LAST CAMPAIGN

Collins' final campaign—a proposal to set up a School of Journalism at Birmingham University—took place in 1907–08, but before coming to this something must be said of his quarrel with the London Extension authorities in 1905–06 (not mentioned by L. C. Collins), which no doubt led to his final break with Extension work in 1907 after twenty-seven years of continuous service. The reason for this quarrel is not all that easy to fathom, but, like other quarrels he provoked during his career, was probably related to his growing conviction that his former friends and allies were now in fact his enemies. As had happened earlier with his uncle, with Swinburne and Gosse, Collins seems to have felt the need to attack the official Extension bodies and to assert his own independence from them, though of course, being Collins, he continued to function as one of their keenest lecturers right up to the end.

The trouble started in the summer of 1905 when Collins began to be difficult in his dealings with the Board to Promote the Extension of University Teaching (the body which took over the functions of the London Society for the Extension of University Teaching in 1902).[1] Collins blithely wrote to the Board saying that he had mislaid his mark book and was therefore unable to say which candidates who had taken his Shakespeare course had qualified for their certificates. This might have been a genuine oversight, yet Collins had never mislaid his mark book before and might now be simply making trouble for the Board. If the Board were in any doubt about this, they were soon aware they had a problem on their hands: Collins asked to meet them to raise some complaints; a meeting was arranged for 6 July, and then cancelled when Collins wrote in to say that he had another engagement that day. The meeting was held shortly afterwards and it appeared that Collins felt that the Board was not providing him with enough opportunities for Extension teaching. (How Collins could have coped with more work than he had remains a mystery.) His chief target here was the Registrar, R. D. Roberts, but after the meeting Collins agreed to drop all his accusations against Roberts.

An uneasy peace continued for a few months, but Collins then renewed his complaints accusing the Registrar and the Board of mismanagement and finding fault with Extension courses and lecturers in general. A letter was sent to Collins from the Board on 7 February 1906, answering his charges one by one in a reasonable but firm tone, and informing him that this was their last word on the subject. It was not their last word, however, because Collins wrote further letters of complaint, one of which contained an 'outrageous' attack on the Registrar. Roberts decided with the Board's approval to place the matter in the hands of his solicitors. The action for libel was brought in April, when Collins, who must have suffered a brainstorm in taking things to these lengths, wrote an abject letter of apology, wholly withdrawing his defamatory statements, expressing his 'sincere regret', and undertaking to pay the costs of bringing the action. This was accepted by Roberts and the matter was dropped.

Collins' relations with official bodies were always apt to be tense and uneasy. Back in 1887, for example, he had had a minor quarrel with the Oxford Extension Committee when it refused to take the stand he wanted on the English issue.[2] This final quarrel with the London Board, however, probably stemmed from his long-simmering dislike of London University, which went back at least as far as his unsuccessful application for the Chair of English at University College in 1889. Collins attacked both King's College and University College in February 1892 for being out of touch with modern education,[3] and in January 1897, in a thinly disguised letter to the *Saturday Review*, strongly criticized the London English courses.[4] Yet again, in March 1899, when London was in the process of being reorganized as a teaching University, he called for the setting up of a 'Department of Higher Civil Education' dealing with vocational and adult education[5] and since this did not eventuate blamed the University for being obstructive and reactionary. In his quarrel with the London Extension Board, Collins was almost certainly carrying on his feud with the university authorities.

2

However, if Oxford and London dragged their feet over the question of educational innovation, Collins was determined to persuade Birmingham to move further in this direction. His co-operation with the Professor of Classics brought his more scholarly ambitions to some kind of fruition, but he still had other ambitions to satisfy, along the lines of his Department of Higher Civil Education. These took shape in his proposal to set up a School of Journalism in the University: such a scheme would provide an education and training suited to the special needs of journalists—something urgently needed in Collins' view—and would also further extend Birmingham University's offerings in the area of useful and relevant studies; the kind of thing Sir Josiah Mason would have approved of. Birmingham already had a School of Commerce; a School of Journalism would be the next obvious step.

Collins first opened the subject on 5 June 1907 when he had an informal meeting with senior colleagues and with the editor of the Birmingham *Daily Post*.[6] All of them were sympathetic and in order to gain further support for the idea, Collins, in his usual way, canvassed opinions from leading journalists and newspaper proprietors. He received replies from such figures as Clement Shorter, founder of the *Sphere*, H. W. Massingham, editor of the *Nation* and Robertson Nicoll, editor of the *British Weekly*. These sent back replies to Collins' questions and were generally encouraging, though one or two doubts were expressed about the feasibility of the scheme. Overall, there was approval for the 'experiment' as something well worth trying and mention was made by Robertson Nicoll of a successful, though less ambitious scheme tried out at the City of London School two years earlier. Of those canvassed, Clement Shorter was the most discouraging saying, 'I do not believe that any London or provincial editor would engage a man on the strength of his having been through such a course as you describe.' Ignoring this negative reply, and taking heart from the rest, Collins pressed forward with his scheme and on 2 July presented his proposals to the University senate. The idea of a School was accepted in principle and a sub-committee set up to draft a specific scheme.

Collins' next move, again following the usual pattern of his campaigning style, was to advertise the scheme in the form of an article entitled 'The Universities and a School of Journalism', which was published in the *Nineteenth Century and After* in February 1908.[7] Here he set out both the theoretical justifications for such a School and the practical proposals for its implementation. As yet, however, it had not been decided whether a full degree course would be set up or whether a shorter postgraduate course would be offered—the decision would depend on the money available. Collins' general justification for a School of Journalism was based on his view of the function of the modern university in society. Forgetting for the moment his creation of a School of English Literature at Birmingham on the lines of his earlier Oxford proposals, he now drew a sharp distinction between the older and the newer universities where function was concerned. Oxford and Cambridge, he argued, were rightly thought of as traditional institutions offering special courses in the Humanities and Classics; they were primarily concerned with education in its accepted sense, rather than with vocational training, and ought not to be taking up subjects like Engineering (already accepted at Oxford) and Agriculture (recently proposed there). The provincial universities, on the other hand, had a responsibility to concern themselves with the needs of modern society and to prepare 'the ordinary citizen . . . for the various avocations open to him'. One of these 'avocations' of course was journalism and there were now good reasons why journalism should take its place alongside other professional subjects in the modern university: 'there is surely as much reason why institutes for advanced secondary education should prepare young men for this profession as for any other profession'. Contemporary journalism, Collins argued with typical gusto, was in a sorry state of confusion, so there was an urgent need to set up properly organized courses in the modern universities which would cater for the academic and professional needs of budding journalists and verify standards:

> Till this is secured it is difficult to see how, as a profession, it can be other than it is, without standards, without principles, without credentials, the general refuge of the canaille and proletariat of the scribbling classes, the realisation of sheer and utter anarchy.[8]

Having delivered this broadside, Collins then outlined the courses so far agreed upon for the projected School.

The scheme consisted of two parts, one academic, the other technical. The academic courses comprised:

Modern English History since 1832.

Modern European History of the last fifty years.

Colonial Affairs (involving political, geographical and social studies).

Political Philosophy (From Burke to Bagehot).

Political Economy.

Finance (National and Municipal systems, Taxation, etc.).

English Literature (special reference to modern literature).

Two Modern Languages (studied for practical purposes).

If necessary, one or two scientific subjects might be studied in place of particular subjects in the above list; and if a postgraduate course only was offered, a selection of four or five of the suggested areas would be studied. The technical side comprised:

Descriptive article writing.

Leading article writing.

Shorthand.

Particular techniques: e.g., the making up of a paper, condensation of news, selection of facts, etc.; management of paragraphs; deciphering and presentation of telegrams and cablegrams.

There would also be instruction in the laws of copyright and libel. The technical side would be taught mainly by practising journalists. Collins concluded his article by reiterating the value of such a scheme and by making an appeal for funds.[9]

Lack of funds, in fact, proved to be the major obstacle to the setting up of the Birmingham School of Journalism, and this time there was no Passmore Edwards around to help out. Collins had been hoping for a full-scale School under the direction of a Professor of Journalism, but in May 1908 was obliged to tell a meeting of journalists and other interested parties that, while the University favoured the idea, lack of money would probably mean indefinite postponement of the scheme. Instead he suggested an alternative, much modified scheme, consisting of a series of lectures and classes over two years for practising journalists, on Modern History, Political Philosophy, Economics and English

Literature.[10] This reduced scheme, costing about £100 p.a. to run, was approved by the University senate in July, with the provision that if insufficient students enrolled to pay for it, the course would not run.[11]

With Collins' death in September, even this reduced scheme suffered a setback and was deferred for another year. The course finally went ahead but the more ambitious aim for a Chair and a School of Journalism was never realized. This was a pity in many ways since the scheme as originally proposed by Collins would have been an important step for both the University and the profession. In the latter case, something had already been done to raise the status of journalism by the founding of the Institute of Journalists in 1890 and the National Union of Journalists in 1907, but little had been done by way of providing schemes for training journalists in professional skills or giving them an education in modern studies appropriate to their needs. Collins' scheme for a School of Journalism would have gone a long way towards giving the profession the kind of status enjoyed by other professions and would also have further strengthened the ties between Birmingham University and the professional and commercial world. Birmingham, in fact, would have been the first British university to give journalism the status it already enjoyed in many American universities.

As had happened before with his various campaigns, Collins could claim only limited success in terms of tangible achievements. Nonetheless—again as happened before—his efforts did not go unrecognized by the profession of journalists. Sir Hugh Gilzean-Reid, founder of the Institute of Journalists, the International Press Union, and the American World's Press Parliament, later wrote to L. C. Collins expressing his regard for Collins' pioneer campaign to raise the status of journalism:

> Only the initiated can fully appreciate the direct and indirect influence which this pioneer action exercised on the movement, both at home and abroad. The name and reputation of the Professor—known and respected in America as well as in Great Britain—acted as a talisman, and was freely used by the journalistic promoters as an authoritative sanction of the principle underlying a scheme which had till then only awakened a professional and academic interest.[12]

So far as Britain was concerned, however, progress in this matter was slow and piecemeal after 1908; diploma courses in journalism were set up by some universities but there was considerable opposition within the profession itself to the whole idea of special training for journalists. J. A. Spender made this point to Collins, when he said 'editors, I am afraid, do not believe in schools of journalism; they believe only in the copy which is delivered to them'.[13] So, despite Gilzean-Reid's enthusiastic response, Collins' scheme also met with some scepticism at the time, though fewer objections could be raised about his proposal for a degree course in modern studies—a genuine Department of Higher Civil Education—which would suit others besides journalists. Unfortunately this was lost along with the School of Journalism but it represented a bold and imaginative idea in 1908. For all his commitment to classical literature, a lifetime as a teacher and spokesman for the Extension movement made Collins sharply aware of other educational priorities.

3

Collins' death in September 1908 was both sudden and mysterious. He left the University in July feeling 'mildly depressed'—no doubt at the reduction in his scheme for journalists—and after visits to Cardiff, where his daughter was lying seriously ill, and Oxford went to stay with his medical adviser and old friend, Dr Daniel, who lived at Oulton Broad, near Lowestoft. At Daniel's house, in the company of friends, he seems to have recovered his spirits: one of his friends there said afterwards: 'I saw Collins many times and for extended periods, generally later on in the day. On all these occasions I found him keen in intellect, brilliant in conversation, sympathetic in temperament. He talked with infectious enthusiasm of the Chair of Journalism which he hoped to see established at Birmingham University. On general topics he was always informative, bright, suggestive.'[14]

Collins left Daniel's house on 12 September, saying that he was going to Weston-super-Mare to join his family. Subsequent events are not clear, but he was last seen alive walking away from the road to the station into the countryside. Three days later his body was found in a shallow dyke, with a bottle of sedatives lying nearby. There was immediate talk of suicide after this sensational discovery, especially since Collins' pocket-book contained the note: 'What will become of my children if I break down. Worries me terribly.' Another entry cryptically stated: 'Enough to provoke suicidal intentions.'[15] But on 18 September a verdict of 'Accidental Death' was returned at the inquest; it was suggested that Collins must have fallen into the dyke under the influence of the sedatives and drowned.[16] Oddly enough, and this added to the air of suspicion surrounding the whole tragic affair, Collins was carrying on him a paper with some disturbingly apposite lines copied out from *Piers Plowman*:

> I was wearie of wandering
> And went me to reste
> Under a brod banke
> Bi a bourne side.
>
> And as I lay and leonede
> And lokede on the waters
> I slumbered in a sleping
> Hit sownede so murie.

All the evidence suggests that Collins had been thinking of suicide, even if he had not exactly intended it. (L. C. Collins, of course, does not entertain this.) Worried and depressed as he was, and with less of his old energy and resilience, Collins seems finally to have just given up the struggle, taking refuge in sedatives—which he had never been known to take before—and giving himself up to whatever might happen. Death may have come accidentally but there is nothing to suggest that Collins actually resisted it. He was buried in the churchyard at Oulton Broad, a world away from the scenes of his hectic campaigns and confrontations—it was a desperately sad climbdown for a man of Collins' fight and stamina.

4

Though Collins clearly had plenty to live for as a Professor at Birmingham—there were always more campaigns to be fought and books to be written—his life, as L. C. Collins says, had really been one long uphill struggle against rejection and failure. His disappointments in applying for university posts, his battles against officialdom of one kind or another, and his general helplessness in the face of what he paranoically came to see as a conspiracy on the part of the literary establishment to promote the second-rate and exclude the best, all in the end wore him down. In his private notebooks, his letters and articles, he always saw himself as the lonely outsider struggling to get things done and principles recognized but generally fighting a losing battle. 'In my humble and quiet way', he told William Watson, speaking of his work for the *Saturday*, 'I have been hammering to get good things read and studied . . . but to lift up my voice at present is but sowing the sand, feeding the wind, darning cobwebs, and whatever else of futility can be practised.'[17] What kept him going was a sense that his mission might come to fruition later; in the preface to *Ephemera Critica*, for example, he wrote, 'I do not suppose that anything I have said will have the smallest effect on the present generation, but on the rising generation I believe that much which has been said will not be thrown away.'[18] At the time of his death, Collins seems to have lost all faith in the future and could only see it in terms of personal failure and disaster.

His death, of course, threw the University of Birmingham into complete disarray, leaving the journalism project without its prime mover, the English Department without its head, and the University without its most popular and liveliest Professor. Everyone was naturally horrified by the news, but the tributes were soon coming in testifying to his personal qualities and achievements. The following from one of his students is typical:

> He always did his best to lighten our work, generally at his own expense. Few of us realised what an enormous amount of work he had to do . . . He did not seem able to take a genuine rest at all, and under stress of work he used to slave for fourteen hours a day, off and on. He was a delightful talker and always put us at our ease, for he seemed to treat everyone as his equal. None of us realised that he was subject to such attacks of depression. To us he was always the same, a genial, sunny, simple and sweet-tempered man, who has and ever will have a place in the hearts of all those who knew him.[19]

Similar tributes were published in *The Times* and other newspapers and in the University Magazine the *Mermaid*; reference was made to Collins' popularity as a teacher, to his phenomenal energy, and to his successful headship of the Birmingham University English Department.[20]

Meanwhile the question of a replacement for Collins was the first urgent requirement at Birmingham—but who could replace Collins, with his special interests and enthusiasm which were strongly felt in every area of university life? If things were to carry on as before, the replacement Professor would need to have an interest in classical and modern European literature, as well as in English literature; he would have to work in close co-operation with the Professor of Classics; and he would have to have an interest in courses for journalists. In the event, in December 1908, the University appointed Ernest de Selincourt to the English Chair, a Professor who had nothing in common with Collins. After taking an Oxford degree in Classics, de Selincourt spent two years studying Old English under Napier before taking up English posts at Bedford College London and at Oxford. With strong interests in textual criticism and bibliography, he belonged to the new generation of English specialists and was expert in fields where Collins was an amateur, but lacked his wide ranging literary passions and interests. He came to Birmingham from the Oxford English School with a high reputation as an editor, and his edition of Keats' Poems in 1905 was described as 'setting a new standard in the editing of a modern poet'.[21]

De Selincourt was an altogether grimmer figure than Collins, without the latter's easy-going relationship with students and with more conventional ideas about English studies; nonetheless in his inaugural lecture he paid generous tribute to his predecessor and to his work for the establishment of English literature as an academic study. Collins, he said, was a great scholar: 'Even among fellow-scholars his reading was accounted enormous—and he had a memory which seemed to retain everything he read.' Collins was also a great campaigner at a time when English literature was taken seriously by very few academics and the fact that things were different now was in large part due to Collins' determined fight:

In the history of the progress of education in the nineteenth century
the name of John Churton Collins stood out as that of a pioneer,
and no one who cared for our great national literature could fail to
recognise the significance of his work.[22]

De Selincourt, however, as might have been expected from one of
Napier's pupils, did not share Collins' enthusiasm for studying
English literature in relation to classical and modern European
literature; as a teacher with experience of the Oxford English
School he wanted English literature studied in its own right, not
as—apparently—an offshoot of a larger literary tradition. Consequently he took immediate steps to modify Collins' English courses
bringing them, as he said, 'more into line with the practice of other
universities'.[23] In the 1909–10 session he made changes which
placed less emphasis upon the relationship between English and
Classics and upon the study of literary theory.[24] He was also
obviously fairly unexcited about Collins' scheme for journalists,
though he agreed to act as general adviser to students enrolling for
these courses.[25]

Collins' comparative approach to the study of literature, then,
did not long survive him at Birmingham and English studies there
seem to have become altogether stricter and duller under de
Selincourt. Official recognition of his abilities as a 'fearless critic'
and of his services to 'English letters' came in the form of a
Memorial organized by a committee of distinguished statesmen,
men of letters and old friends and acquaintances, including
Asquith, Lord Curzon, Viscount Morley, Conan Doyle, Beerbohm
Tree (admired by Collins for his encouragement of Stephen
Phillips), several bishops and vice-chancellors, and many others.
Swinburne and Gosse were conspicuously absent. The committee
received a large number of donations and presented sums of
money to Oxford, Cambridge and London to set up 'Churton
Collins Prizes' for 'the encouragement of the study of English and/
or Classical Literature among University Extension Students and
others.' Birmingham University received a sum of money for an
annual 'Churton Collins Memorial Prize' for English and/or
Classical Literature. Specially bound sets of Collins' books were
presented to Balliol College, the University of Leeds (his old friend
Sir Nathan Bodington was Vice-Chancellor there), King Edward's

School Birmingham, and the Wolverhampton Literary Club, of which Collins was the first President.[26]

It was all a tamely official conclusion to Collins' career, though in true Collinsian fashion the Memorial proceedings had their own touch of controversy. Theodore Watts-Dunton, Swinburne's chief friend and custodian, was asked to take the chair on the Memorial committee on the grounds that he was a long-standing acquaintance of Collins as well as being competent in such matters. Watts-Dunton, still nursing his anger at Collins for the unprovoked attack on Swinburne more than twenty years earlier, curtly refused but did agree to sign the memorial for Mrs Churton Collins' pension, granted in 1909. Swinburne heartlessly refused to do even that.[27] Thus, in a minor way, the controversies stirred up by Collins during his lifetime continued fitfully and spitefully after his death.

NOTES

1   The details of this affair are recorded in the *Minutes* of the University of London Board to Promote the Extension of University Teaching, May 1905 to May 1906. University of London Library.

2   See above, p. 76.

3   J. C. Collins, 'The Ideal University', *Nineteenth Century*, XXXI, February 1892, pp. 243–54.

4   *Saturday Review*, 30 January 1897, p. 119.

5   J. C. Collins, 'A University for the People', *Nineteenth Century*, XLV, March 1899, pp. 465–76.

6   See L. C. Collins, op. cit., pp. 257 ff.

7   J. C. Collins, 'The Universities and a School of Journalism', *Nineteenth Century and After*, LXIII, February 1908, pp. 327–40.

8   Ibid., p. 337.

9   Ibid., pp. 338–40.

10 Birmingham *Daily Post*, 20 May 1908.

11 Ibid., 9 July 1908.

12 L. C. Collins, op. cit., p. 276.

13 Ibid., p. 264.

14 Ibid., p. 286.

15 *The Times*, 16 September 1908, p. 11.

16 Ibid., 18 September 1908, p. 11.

17 L. C. Collins, op. cit., p. 140.

18 *Ephemera Critica*, p. 7.

19 L. C. Collins, op. cit., p. 185.

20 See, for example, the obituary notices in *The Times*, 17 September 1908, p. 9, and the *Mermaid*, November 1908, pp. 16–17.

21 See D. S. Brewer, op. cit., p. 25.

22 Birmingham *Daily Post*, 13 October 1909.

23 *Report* of the Dean of the Faculty of Arts 1908–09, p.7.

24 Faculties of Science, Arts and Commerce *Regulations and Syllabuses* 1909–10, pp. 77–79 and 239–42.

25 L. C. Collins, op. cit., p. 279.

26 Ibid., pp. 312–15.

27 This information is contained in an undated MS. letter from Theodore Watts-Dunton to T. J. Wise. Brotherton Library, University of Leeds.

CHAPTER TEN

SUMMING UP

As a propagandist for literature and literary studies, Collins plainly saw himself following the example of Matthew Arnold, though contemporaries of course found contrasts rather than similarities between the two. The *Spectator* reviewer of Collins' *The Study of English Literature*, for example, contrasted his 'almost forensic tone' with Arnold's urbanity in dealing with opponents: 'we are irresistibly led to reflect how differently that great controversialist, Matthew Arnold, would have directed hostilities against a common foe. With what urbane raillery he would have demoralised their ranks; with what exquisite torture he would have agonized his victims and entertained the world at large; with what seemingly careless precision, and what intolerable affability, he would have run his rapier through his enemy's vitals.'[1] Whatever the contrasts in approach and style, however, Collins' indebtedness to Arnold's ideas and to his particular formulations is unmistakable.

Arnold, for Collins, was first of all the great analyst of the age; the keen-eyed searcher out of its defects and failings. In May 1892, speaking to the students at Gresham College of the English lack of perception where the harmonious was concerned, Collins went on to say

> Now from this radical defect spring most of our characteristic vices as a nation. You know that Matthew Arnold has analyzed these vices and defects for us. He says that, on the side of beauty and taste we are distinguished by *vulgarity*, on the side of morality and feeling we are distinguished by *coarseness*, and on the side of mind and spirit we are distinguished by *unintelligence*.[2]

The remedy proposed was also Arnold's: namely the acquisition of Hellenic sweetness and light through a study of Greek literature and Greek ideals. Like Arnold Collins constantly used the Greeks in this tendentious way to point up the parochial absurdities of Victorian society, and, not least of all, its educational aims and practices. In his book *Greek Influence on English Poetry*, for example, he wrote—again following Arnold—

> They (i.e. the Greeks) directed education to its proper ends, the development, the culture, the discipline of those instincts and faculties which enable, or tend to enable, a man to secure the greatest possible happiness for himself, and by implication for all who are associated with him in all the various relations of domestic and political life. They did not subordinate what is proper for the man and the citizen to what is proper for the specialist and mere scholar who are needed, are indeed indispensable, in every civilized community, but who after all do not perform the highest function in the work of education ... With what pitying contempt would that large sane intelligence have regarded our Baconian-Shakespeare controversies, our editions of Shakespeare's plays copiously annotated with a view to various examinations, our Mediaeval and Modern Languages Triposes, our text-books and Examination papers on English history and English Literature![3]

Secondly Arnold, along with Carlyle, had done more than any other contemporary to insist on the ethical and spiritual values of great poetry which provided the main basis for Collins' earnest campaigns for literature in education. Finally, of course, there was Arnold the great critic teaching the age the truest standards:

> how great, how salutary were his services to criticism. He taught it measure, sobriety, lucidity, precision. He derived his canons from the habitual, discriminating, and sympathetic study of all that was most excellent in the literature of ancient Greece and Rome, of modern Italy, of England, of France, of Germany ... His judgment was a very Ithuriel's spear in the detection of what was spurious and unsound ... with what piercing truth he explains the essential difference between poetry of the first order and poetry of the second order, the differences which separate Chaucer from Homer, and Dryden from Wordsworth ...[4]

Yet, despite his genuine admiration for Arnold the literary propagandist and critic, Collins' personality was too different from Arnold's for him to approve everything about the man. In his interesting late essay on Arnold, from which the last quotation is taken, Collins qualified his respect for Arnold's intelligence, sensitivity and insight by pointing to certain faults in his make-up; he was a great critic, but no Reformer or Teacher; he was too timid and fastidious to achieve anything in the world of literature and education:

> But here he failed in character; he was not made of the stuff out of which Reformers are made. He had no enthusiasm: nothing of the magnetism which intensity of conviction and intensity of purpose inspire: he was timid, sensitive, and self-conscious, afraid of ridicule, and especially of the ridicule which earnestness and emphasis so easily excite in 'superior people'.[5]

Arnold, in other words, as a prophet and reformer lacked Carlyle's *force*—the force so admired by Collins himself.

This of course was not only a portrait of Arnold, but a self-portrait too by implication. Collins was the intense and earnest campaigner for Arnold's ideals and his whole career was taken up fighting what he thought of as Arnold's battles, seeing himself in moments of self-idealization in the light of his two political heroes Demosthenes and Burke, men who 'animated by the purest motives, patriots to the innermost fibre, with no thought, with no aim but for the public good, wore out their lives in leading forlorn hopes and fighting losing battles'.[6] Arnold, on the other hand, through lack of real conviction and courage, had preferred to remain on the sidelines talking of sweetness and light. Collins, of course, conveniently forgot that he had elsewhere applauded Arnold's Hellenic detachment as a model for the age.

His later mixed feelings about Arnold, however, stemmed from a private disappointment. In October 1886, as his Oxford campaign for a new School of Literature began to get under way, Collins naturally turned to Arnold for encouragement and support. Arnold's response—in the form of three letters—however was decidedly cautious. He told Collins that he was in favour of adding some English works to the existing classical syllabuses at Oxford but was not in favour of a new School of Literature on the lines suggested by Collins.[7] Arnold obviously felt that a separate School for the conjoint study of English and Classical literature was too radical a step. He told Collins that Oxford had seen too many reforms and experiments during the previous forty years and that he had 'no confidence in those who at the Universities regulate, degrees, and honours'.[8]

Apart from his educational principles, Arnold was also clearly wary of Collins' campaign on other grounds. Not least of all he disliked the way Collins had dragged Gosse into the dispute. In his first letter Arnold told Collins 'I am unwilling to appear in a question which is mixed up with the question of the merits of Mr Gosse . . . If it is possible to intervene with any good effect later, and when the question is cleared of Mr Gosse, pray communicate with me.'[9] Arnold understandably was not going to get caught up in any of Collins' private quarrels. At the same time one can also understand Collins' own sense of betrayal. Gosse apart, he felt he was fighting for Arnold's causes and expected stronger support than was manifestly forthcoming. His disappointment with Arnold surfaced in a typically scathing letter to the *Pall Mall Gazette* shortly afterwards:

> As for Mr Matthew Arnold we all know him; we all know that Protean temper and that Protean wit: poet, theologian, critic, 'greatest living authority on education', dilettante, what is he, what is he not? . . . For the last twenty years he has figured as the apostle of culture; he has been dinning into our ears that we are Philistines; he has been bewailing the degradation of current literature, he has been groaning over our insensibility to what is excellent in art and criticism, but when there is a chance of aiding a movement which, if successful, will go far to remedy what he deplores, he prefers to fold his arms and talk about 'lost causes' when he is trifling, and 'instincts of self-preservation in humanity' when he is eloquent.[10]

Collins' recognition of Arnold's significance as a critic never really faltered but for years afterwards Arnold's half-hearted support of the Oxford campaign continued to rankle. The only time he softened towards Arnold the man was, typically, when he thought of his personal sorrows and tragedies: Arnold's services as a school inspector met with little recognition, much of his life was spent in 'repulsive drudgery' with little time for 'more congenial pursuits', he had little money 'and, if not actually poor, [was] always grazing embarrassment'; yet despite these difficulties and the loss of 'loved children' 'he was never other than cheerful, genial, playful, and uncomplaining, the most delightful of companions, the most affectionate of husbands, of fathers, and of friends'.[11]

In the end Collins' active polemics and campaigning were necessary if Arnold's literary and educational ideals were to be given practical effect. Someone had to rouse the classicists, involve the Extension Movement, answer the philologists and the sceptics and present a powerfully argued case for taking English literature seriously as an academic study at the highest levels, and Collins rather than Arnold was the man to do all this. Arnold, in fact, never fully committed himself to the idea of English literature as a university study: like most of his generation his main concern was to preserve Classics; English literature might well develop as a major study in the training colleges and the elementary schools— and Arnold's school reports insisted that it should at these levels— but in university education could only be thought of as an adjunct to Classics. Finally it was left to Collins to marshal all the arguments for placing English literature firmly in the university curriculum, and this he did persuasively enough for his book *The Study of English Literature* to become a standard work on the subject. Nearly thirty years later indeed when the English Tripos was being set up at Cambridge, Collins' book was still being used by the English propagandists. Writing of these times, Tillyard says, 'With some modifications (principally to do with the rigid insistence on the background) Collins' book might have served as the text for the principles on which the English Tripos was founded in 1917. And indeed it had its influence, because Forbes knew it and advertised its doctrines.'[12]

2

The 'modifications' which Tillyard says were necessary in Collins' idea of an English School related of course to his emphasis on the Classical influence. Collins, notoriously, exaggerated the indebtedness of English literature to Classical (though to be fair he qualified his argument by limiting the influence to poetry in the main, and to 'what is most valuable in English poetry' at that).[13] With his enthusiasm for Classical literature and his staggering memory for quotations, he was inevitably carried away by his echoes and parallels into a distorted view of English literature, or at least into a view which either had to exclude parts of it as unclassical and therefore less 'valuable', or else make out a case for the Classical influence where it was unlikely—for example in Shakespeare. Much of his argument for the Classical influence came down in the end to great minds thinking alike and even expressing themselves alike, though at times, for example in his *Illustrations of Tennyson*, Collins was able to offer more convincing arguments for direct influence. As for the more general case, no one could deny that a large number of English writers from Chaucer to the nineteenth century had been reared on the Classics and had been indirectly, if not directly, influenced by them, but it was plainly nonsensical to say, as Collins did, that no proper study of English literature was possible without a knowledge of these connexions.

Despite this idiosyncratic over-emphasis, Collins' attempt to link English and Classics did have its rationale and support in the 1880s. His proposal for a new School of Literature in fact marked an important stage in the evolution of English studies which offered both English and Classics a new life and respectability in education. For those of Collins' generation brought up on Classics and with an interest in English literature, his suggestion of a working alliance between the two subjects seemed both natural and politic, a means of grafting English on to an established subject and of exploring relationships between different literatures and cultures. Those concerned with the future of literature in education naturally looked to the Classical alliance as offering a broader and more humane model for literary studies than the philological one and Collins' Extension courses and his Birmingham English reforms were a practical working out of this idea. Intelligent Classics teachers like Sonnenschein at Birmingham also realized that this offered the most promising prospect for Classics; as the Board of Education Report, *The Teaching of English in England*, put it in 1921, 'Classical studies would be in a securer position today if their teachers had always recognized that the study of English literature was an essential supplement to them.'[14]

Collins, of course, always saw himself as a teacher of 'literature' rather than 'English literature' but to those not brought up on the ideals of Arnold and Jowett, or out of sympathy with them, Collins' approach seemed of more benefit to Classics than English. For a new generation of teachers and students, the exploration of links between Classical and English literature came to look more and more a specialist concern and not part of a general literary education. Even before Collins' death in 1908, new campaigners were demanding an independent status for English literature as an academic subject without alliances or supports from Classics or Philology, and within a few years students were able to study the subject on its own. The ideal English School, in the eyes of the Committee set up after the First World War to consider the position of English in education, was one dependent neither on Classics nor Philology, though these aspects might be provided for by special options; it was a School where the main emphasis was on the study of modern (i.e. post-Chaucerian) literature as literature.[15]

Collins' ideas then were soon overtaken by new developments, but for a short period between about 1880 and 1910 English studies in the universities were delicately poised between Classical and Philological interests. It is to his credit that he made the former interest a practical possibility which for all its over-emphasis on the influence of Classical literature on English literature did at least make literature a central concern and helped to rescue both Classics and English from the worst excesses of arid teaching. Collins' approach to the teaching of literature, which appealed to thousands of Extension and university students over the years, clearly represented the healthiest attitude to the subject at the time.

Nor, of course, was he so besotted by classical ideals, by Oxford and by Arnold, that he was out of touch with wider educational issues. No one involved himself more in new educational projects and experiments and from about 1880 until his death Collins was more or less continuously engaged in educational campaigns for new Extension courses, for new schools of literature, for new literature syllabuses and for new ventures such as the School of Journalism. In a way it was lucky he ended up at Birmingham rather than Oxford; at Birmingham he found ready listeners and supporters for his various enterprises; at Oxford, one imagines, he would have quickly lost his radical enthusiasms in a climate of caution and conservatism. In some ways it would have been even better for him to have gone to an American university like his Extension colleague R. G. Moulton who took the Chair of

Literature at Chicago in 1894. Collins, according to L. C. Collins, was in fact offered a chair at Baltimore, probably during his visit to America in 1894, but declined it.[16] In America he would have found stronger support, and more generous funds, for his schemes than he found in England, even at Birmingham, but he was far too committed to England, its literature and culture to emigrate.

3

Collins the literary scholar and critic is a simpler matter to deal with than Collins the educational campaigner. During his career he wrote twelve books (two appearing posthumously) and about fifty literary articles and edited twenty-four works, not counting of course a vast amount of reviewing and miscellaneous journalism. The weakest side of all this work was the editing and, as has already been seen, his major editions—*Plays and Poems of Cyril Tourneur* (1878), *Poems of Lord Herbert of Cherbury* (1881) and *Plays and Poems of Robert Greene* (1905)—though prepared with love and care were all later criticized for carelessness. Where settling the text was not at issue, Collins' editions of English classics fared better and his editions of Milton's *Samson Agonistes* (1883), Pope's *Essay on Criticism* (1896) and Sidney's *Apologie for Poetrie* (1907) survived for several generations of students, mainly for their clear and readable introductions. Collins was also a successful general editor of Arnold's 'School Shakespeare' where as might be expected he took a firm anti-philological line; in the words of a reviewer, 'Mr Churton Collins's design is to enable students to make a liberal study of Shakespeare, regarded from a literary and historical rather than from a grammatical and philological standpoint.'[17]

Apart from his editing, Collins' literary work was generally accepted at the time as learned, incisive and competent, though often of course marred by overstatement and assertiveness. What Arnold said of Macaulay's style—a 'style brilliant, metallic, exterior; making strong points, alternating invective with eulogy, wrapping in a robe of rhetoric the thing it represents'[18]—could be said of Collins' and he was always being told by reviewers to 'prune away excess and study balance with force'.[19] For contem-

poraries, Collins' best books were those where he was neither
attacking enemies, as in *Ephemera Critica*, nor chasing the classical
influence, as in *Studies in Shakespeare*, but following up his interests
in biography and history. He was at his most objective (though
never overly so) in his studies of Bolingbroke, Voltaire, Swift,
Montesquieu and Rousseau—these at any rate were the books his
contemporaries most admired and which still from time to time get
mentioned.[20] Collins as biographer and critic was certainly the
equal of contemporaries like Stephen and Morley and, in terms of
accuracy, far superior to the likes of Gosse and Saintsbury, but his
reputation as a serious writer suffered inevitably from his constant
argufying.

Collins always regretted the fact that his various pressing
commitments never left him the time to engage in large-scale
research projects (such things as a continuation of Macaulay's
History of England and a study of the literary relationship
between England and France in the eighteenth century), so that
all he achieved were small-scale versions of what might have been
larger works. This no doubt was sad and unfortunate, yet one
suspects that Collins, when it came down to it, really preferred
short pieces of research produced for some specific purpose, a
lecture, an essay or a review. This was certainly the kind of work he
excelled at and his most memorable writing, whatever contemporaries felt about it, was his reviewing where the sense of occasion
and the prospect of an argument always brought out his best
debating skills. As a reviewer he was a man of some literary
consequence, wielding a good deal of power in precisely the way
he liked, and in terms of being sharp, alert and frighteningly
industrious (Le Gallienne's 'demon-mole') Collins had no equals
on the late Victorian reviewing scene. His reviews naturally
infuriated and upset a good many notable authors of the time but
for those not under attack they not only made out forceful and
damning cases but also provided the liveliest and most entertaining reading of the day. Who else but Collins, for example, would
have concluded a review of a Saintsbury book by referring to 'the
mingled coarseness, triviality and dogmatism of his tone, the
audacious nonsense of his generalisations, and the offensive vul-
garity of his diction and style'?[21] Collins, of course, often went
right over the top in his condemnation of particular works, but in

his own naive and sincere way he wanted to make reviewing a matter of plain, blunt speaking; after all, speaking out was his main mission in life. It is also worth pointing out that while he was often carried away by the sound of his own voice he rarely indulged himself in personal attacks on the writers themselves— the main exceptions here being the attacks on Gosse, the Clark Lecturer, and Saintsbury, the Edinburgh Professor. In terms of being straightforwardly abusive, Collins was a mere novice in comparison with a contemporary like Swinburne.

When Collins liked a book he also said so in the same assertive way, though the usual account of him suggests that he was always on the attack. The opening of his review of Sidney Lee's *Life of Shakespeare*, reprinted in *Ephemera Critica*, is a case in point:

> It is a pleasure to turn from the slovenly and perfunctory work, from the plausible charlatanry and pretentious incompetence which it has so often been our unwelcome duty to expose in these columns [i.e. in the *Saturday Review*], to such a volume as the volume before us. It is books like these which retrieve the honour of English scholarship. A wide range of general knowledge, immense special knowledge, scrupulous accuracy, both in the investigation and presentation of facts, the sound judgment, the tact, the insight which in labyrinths of chaotic traditions and conflicting testimony can discern the clue to probability and truth—these are the qualifications indispensable to a successful biographer of Shake-speare. And these are the qualifications which Mr Lee possesses, in larger measure than have been possessed by any one who has essayed the task which he has here undertaken.[22]

This of course is another rebuke for Saintsbury and Gosse as well as a compliment to Lee. Lee, it has to be admitted, was on friendly terms with Collins (he later wrote the biographical note on Collins for the *Dictionary of National Biography*),[23] but there is no disputing the fact that Collins admired the good solid Pattison-like virtues of Lee's book. Moreover, as if to prove the point that he was offering an honest not a flattering account of the book, Collins found some faults with Lee's ineptness as a literary critic: 'Mr Lee must also forgive us for adding that, in this work at least, aesthetic criticism is not his strong point, and he would have done well to keep it within even narrower bounds than he has done.'[24] But Lee's book overall met with Collins' firm approval; it was a sober and conscientious work with none of the breezy superficiality and stylistic self-indulgence which offended him in the work of Symonds, Gosse and Saintsbury, not to mention Raleigh and aesthetes like Le Gallienne.

4

Opinions of Collins the man and the critic varied widely after his death. The most hostile views of course came from those who had either been directly attacked by him or who were friends of those who had. References to 'Shirt 'n Collars' and 'the louse on the locks of literature' were common in the Gosse–Swinburne–Watts-Dunton circle during Collins' lifetime and after his death became part of his legend. Theodore Watts-Dunton provided the most virulent comment on Collins in a letter to T. J. Wise, describing him as 'a pretentious decidedly inferior person'. 'After his quarrel with Gosse', Watts-Dunton continued, 'he got Lady Dilke to invite me expressly to meet him. I told him frankly that he was the most envious malignant man in Great Britain.'[25] Watts-Dunton was even more furious when Collins attacked Swinburne, and though he contrived to bring about the last ill-fated meeting between the two men in February 1900 on Collins' insistence, he never forgave Collins for his abuse of Swinburne's friendship and patronage and evidently took a leading role in the moves to blacken his reputation. Collins, of course, made it easy for his enemies to create their image of him as the 'Timon of critics' (Arthur Symons' tag),[26] a man so eaten up by envy and bitterness that he would stop at nothing to destroy the reputations of successful men of letters. Episodes like the Symonds and Gosse reviews, books like *The Study of English Literature* and *Ephemera Critica* and the gossip of literary circles all helped to give notoriety to Collins and account for his popular image today as 'the brooding assassin' and the 'scourge' of the late Victorians.[27]

Equally, however, as is made very plain in L. C. Collins' biography, there were many approving opinions of Collins particularly from students, colleagues and those who knew him well over a number of years. These vied with each other in highlighting his excellent personal qualities, his kindness, honesty, generosity and loyalty—qualities which must have been evident to Swinburne and Gosse too in the early days of their friendship with Collins. Frank Harris, for example, in his attractive portrait of Collins as he knew him on the *Saturday Review*, described him as follows:

> He lived in this way to me for several years, as a solid, strong, capable teacher of English literature, with wide reading, a bad memory [sic!], and a surpassing carefulness about mere facts; an honest, kindly nature, full of chivalry and loyalty, with incomprehensible bitterness towards what he regarded as pretentious ignorance; a good and cheery host, an easily pleased and laughter-loving guest, preferring his pipe and armchair and a good talk about letters (poetry for choice) to anything in the world.[28]

Harris's portrait is duplicated many times in the pages of L. C. Collins' book, in the obituary notices, and in various reports and comments made on Collins from time to time. With all his talent for breaking old relationships and making enemies, he managed to retain the friendship and affection of many more people than might be supposed. Collins for many of his contemporaries was far from being the ogre of Victorian letters.

Other opinions of Collins, from people who knew him less well or not at all, concerned his abilities rather than his personality and tended towards the view that he was a sound scholar rather than a literary critic. For Arnold Bennett, for example, his learning was the most impressive thing about him: 'I should suppose that on the subject of literature he was the most learned man in Britain.'[29] The same view was echoed by later readers of Collins' books. Desmond MacCarthy, for instance, made the same point when looking at his *Illustrations of Tennyson*: 'What learning! one exclaims as one reads it, and—with greater astonishment—what a memory! For Churton Collins belonged to the old school of bookmen who carried their learning about with them, not to the type of the latter-day literary man, who is unable to quote fifty consecutive lines of Homer or Shakespeare, but keeps his erudition on the shelves.'[30] Bennett, however, felt that Collins, with all his erudition, was 'quite bereft of original taste':

> The root of the matter was not in him. The frowning structure of his vast knowledge overawed many people, but it never overawed

an artist—unless the artist was excessively young and naive. A man may heap up facts on a given topic, and assort and label them, and have the trick of producing any particular fact at an instant's notice, and yet, despite all his efforts and toil, rest hopelessly among the profane.[31]

This of course is Collins the demon-mole again—the persecutor of the Le Galliennes—and represents a distorted view of the man and his work. Collins, however much a stickler for accuracy where facts and details were concerned, was certainly no mere accumulator of literary data; he had as many opinions as facts to display and his critical writings were always too lively and forceful to fit Bennett's description of him as a laborious and tasteless pedant. Bennett as a creative writer had a strong dislike of literary professors (he dismissed Saintsbury and Raleigh in a similar way in his piece on Collins) and was clearly indulging his prejudices in setting Collins down as a learned hack.

Yet, despite Bennett's obvious bias, Collins did have his manifest limitations as a critic. According to his own Arnoldian view of the matter, the literary critic needed to have 'rare power of analysis, the nicest perception, sensibility, sympathy, good taste, good sense, immense erudition';[32] Collins clearly had some of these desirable qualities—powers of analysis, good sense and erudition—but lacked others, particularly sympathy (unless confronted by a struggling genius). As a teacher of literature, he tended to think too exclusively in terms of preconceived categories of 'greatness' and 'limitation' and, like Arnold, was fond of classifying writers in fixed ranks—thus he saw writers like Chaucer, Dryden, Pope, Byron and Shelley more in terms of their failure to achieve true greatness than as writers with their own individual qualities and achievements.[33] In his obvious eagerness to classify and judge Collins often fell into the trap referred to by R. G. Moulton in his warning about the hazards of 'judicial criticism'. This sort of critical approach, said Moulton, could in itself be 'a barrier to appreciation, as being opposed to that delicacy of receptiveness which is a first condition of sensibility to impressions of literature and art'.[34] Collins, with his vast knowledge of literary traditions, influences and connexions, was always the learned reader and this tended to make him a dictatorial critic and reviewer. Like other judicial critics he was unreceptive to new movements and voices and when dealing with modern writers preferred poets like William Watson and Stephen Phillips, who could be assimilated to acceptable poetic traditions, to the new breed of nineties poets. On the whole his jaundiced view of modern literature meant that he did not move much beyond the safe limits of Tennyson, Browning and Swinburne and he had nothing to say about poets like Symons and Yeats. Bennett said that Collins displayed 'in acute degree the characteristic inability of the typical professor to toddle alone when released from the leading strings of tradition'[35] and, despite the sneering tone, he was basically right. Like Arnold, yet again, Collins was mainly interested in poetry as the most significant literary form and made scarcely any reference to novelists in his writings (no George Eliot, Hardy or Gissing), though he enjoyed Dickens and knew the ending of *Dombey and Son* by heart.[36]

5

Collins the man is not easy to come at behind the contradictory images he succeeded in creating for himself during his career as critic and campaigner, but among his best points can be included his intellectual and critical honesty, his consistency of principle, his forthrightness and his determination. No fair-minded contemporary ever questioned his possession of these qualities. Collins was certainly too extreme in his handling of particular issues but this normally came from his obsessive sense of mission as a truth-teller and critic rather than from sheer destructiveness (though of course there were significant exceptions to this rule). His main difficulties and problems came from his deep unease and anxiety about himself, his own life and career; his feeling that with all his achievements he had never really received the rewards and recognition he deserved. This eventually developed into a paranoid belief that the literary and academic establishments had closed ranks to exclude and oppose him (which, on the whole, of course was not true). This made him more aggressive, self-justifying and bitter than he otherwise would have been; it complicated most of his relationships and made his life a protracted series of conflicts. To his closest friends and colleagues he showed genuine warmth, affection and generosity—his students also saw this side of him. But he also felt constantly threatened by a succession of enemies (some of them former friends like Swinburne and Gosse) who seemed to stand in the way of his progress towards self-fulfilment and success. This in turn led to sharp confrontations rationalized—partly justifiably—as stands for particular rights and principles. Collins in this way bears some similarity to Gissing's Alfred Yule, an idealistic literary man but embittered by years of frustrating struggle and lack of success and driven to agonizing self-reflections: 'From my boyhood', Yule tells his daughter, 'I have had a passionate desire of literary fame, deep down below all the surface faults of my character. The best of my life has gone by, and it drives me to despair when I feel that I have not gained the position due to me.'[37] This, up to a point, might be Collins commiserating with himself in the pages of his private notebook.

But only up to a point: Collins in reality was no downtrodden failure like Alfred Yule, despite his share of Yule's bitterness with the metropolitan literary world. Notwithstanding his frustrations and disappointments in particular directions—the Oxford English chairs, the Oxford English School and the full-scale School of Journalism at Birmingham—he managed to make a gratifyingly strong impact as a teacher, campaigner and reviewer and achieved an un-Yule like status as a respected spokesman and propagandist on literary and cultural affairs. Collins' real place in the literary and educational world of his time, indeed, was similar in many respects to that occupied by F. R. Leavis fifty years later. Though Leavis knew little of Collins' life and work, thought little of him as a scholar-critic and would have violently objected to the comparison,[38] the two men did have certain striking things in common: both were actively engaged in campaigning for particular approaches to English in education (Mansfield Forbes' liking for Collins' *The Study of English Literature* is relevant here), both attacked the university and literary establishments of their time, both struggled for many years against official disapproval and discouragement, and both were outspoken reviewers constantly involved in controversy. Leavis, it goes without saying, was a much greater critic than Collins and, through *Scrutiny*, more influential as a propagandist; nonetheless the similarities are obvious enough.

Both Collins and Leavis as teachers and critics helped to transmit Arnold's literary and cultural ideas to their respective audiences and readers and both strongly defended literary standards against academic as well as popular and commercial devaluations. Despite the obvious differences of period and literary preference, which make Collins look decidedly the old-fashioned bookman when set beside Leavis, the writings which make up Collins' *Ephemera Critica* and *The Study of English Literature* have much in common with Leavis's *Education and the University* and *Nor Shall My Sword*: in both men there was the same strong urge to confront a whole range of opponents—university academics, metropolitan literary cliques, publishers, second-rate critics, and the like—the same sense of cultural crisis and the same call for a reassertion of traditional values. Collins was blunter, cruder, more self-displaying as a critic and propagandist than Leavis—Leavis was a much more scrupulous and courteous controversialist—but both essentially were fighting on the same side for similar things. The comparison is flattering to Collins but it helps to indicate the kind of importance he had in his own time.

This importance is easily confirmed when we remember the respect given him by major figures of the period, including some of course who later fell out with him. Jowett, Pattison and many others were deeply impressed by his knowledge of Classical and modern literature; Swinburne discussed poetry with him and took his opinions of it seriously; Leslie Stephen (much admired by Q. D. Leavis), Andrew Lang and Edward Dowden all praised him as a historian, critic and biographer; Symonds, Gosse and Saintsbury were forced to acknowledge his battery of facts even if they disliked his style of reviewing; Goschen along with everyone else in the Extension hierarchy admired his skill and flair as a teacher; the literary world called him a 'new Macaulay'; leading newspaper editors and proprietors took his idea for a School of Journalism at least half seriously; and a variety of distinguished politicians, churchmen and literary figures listened to him and supported his different causes. All this suggests that, with all his faults, his overstatements, his assertiveness, his stridency and instability, he was something more than the demon-mole and the louse on the locks of literature of popular mythology.

NOTES

1   The *Spectator*, 5 March 1892, pp. 334–35.
2   This lecture was published in the *University Extension Journal*, 15 June 1892, pp. 80–82.
3   *Greek Influence on English Poetry*, pp. 18–19.
4   *The Posthumous Essays of John Churton Collins*, pp. 196–97.
5   Ibid., p. 172.
6   Ibid., p. 50.
7   Arnold's three letters to Collins dated 24 October 1886, 4 December 1886 and 29 December 1886 were privately printed in *Letters from Matthew Arnold to John Churton Collins*, 1910, a limited edition of twenty copies.
8   Ibid., 29 December 1886.
9   Ibid., 4 December 1886.
10 *Pall Mall Gazette*, 8 December 1886, pp. 11–12.
11 *The Posthumous Essays of John Churton Collins*, pp. 177–78.
12 *The Muse Unchained*, p. 32. The reference here is to Mansfield Forbes, the most active of the campaigners for the Cambridge English Tripos. For an interesting account of Forbes see F. R. Leavis, *English Literature in Our Time and the University*, 1969, pp. 14 ff.
13 See *The Study of English Literature*, p. 154.
14 *The Teaching of English in England*, H.M.S.O., 1921, p. 209.
15 Ibid., pp. 226–29.
16 L. C. Collins, op. cit., p. 174.
17 *Saturday Review*, 5 September 1896, p. 236.
18 Matthew Arnold, *Mixed Essays*, 1879, p. 238.
19 The words of a reviewer in the *Academy*, 23 November 1895, pp. 427–28.
20 Collins' books *Bolingbroke and Voltaire in England* and *Voltaire, Montesquieu and Rousseau in England* for example are both listed in the bibliography of Charles Vereker's *Eighteenth Century Optimism*, Liverpool, 1967, p. 310.
21 *Ephemera Critica*, p. 109.
22 Ibid., p. 211.
23 Lee was someone Collins consulted and confided in and they often met socially. See L. C. Collins, op. cit., pp. 144–46, 162, 304 and 313. See also Collins' four letters to Lee in the *Correspondence of Sir Sidney Lee* in the Bodleian Library.
24 *Ephemera Critica*, p. 218.
25 Undated MS letter from Theodore Watts-Dunton to T. J. Wise. Brotherton Library, University of Leeds.

26 *Fortnightly Review*, LXXV, June 1901, p. 1004.

27 See respectively, John Gross, op. cit., p. 177 and Phyllis Grosskurth, 'Churton Collins: Scourge of the Late Victorians', *University of Toronto Quarterly*, 34, April 1965, pp. 254–68.

28 Frank Harris, op. cit., p. 314.

29 Arnold Bennett, *Books and Persons*, 1917, p. 32.

30 Desmond MacCarthy, *Experience*, 1935, p. 278.

31 Arnold Bennett, op. cit., p.32.

32 *Ephemera Critica*, pp. 203–04.

33 See for example, Collins' classification and ranking of poets in his article 'Can English Literature be Taught?', *Nineteenth Century*, XXII, November 1887, p. 657.

34 R. G. Moulton, *Shakespeare as a Dramatic Artist*, Oxford, 1885, p. 6.

35 Arnold Bennett, op. cit., pp. 32–33. A similar view of Collins the Professorial critic was expressed by W. B. Yeats. See *Uncollected Prose* by W. B. Yeats, edited by J. P. Frayne and Colton Johnson, 2 vols. 1975, II, 293–94.

36 L. C. Collins, op. cit., p. 221. The surprising omission here is Gissing; one would have expected Collins to have been drawn to Gissing's moving portrayals of the struggles of authors, adult education lecturers and the like.

37 George Gissing, *New Grub Street*, Penguin edition, 1968, pp. 352–53.

38 In correspondence with me, Leavis said that he knew of only one book by Collins—the Swift biography—and that he thought Collins' significance to be negligible. This suggests that Leavis knew very little about earlier phases of the battle for English in the universities.

COLLINS' MARRIAGE

L. C. Collins refers to his father's marriage very briefly and circumspectly as follows: 'Meanwhile he had met and married my mother, then Pauline Mary Strangways, only daughter of Thomas Henry Strangways and cousin of the Honourable H. B. Strangways, at whose fine old manor at Shapwick, Somerset, my father and mother regularly spent part of their holiday every year—a visit which he always enjoyed and which did him much good.'[1] Thereafter there are few references in the biography to Collins' wife or to their personal and domestic relationship, though clearly Pauline Collins had a great deal to put up with, what with her husband's chronic depression, an uncertain income and eventually a family of seven children to bring up. Brief references in Collins' notebooks, however, together with some in the biography, suggest both his strong attachment to his wife and his sense of guilt in causing her various problems. Some sample entries in the notebooks give glimpses of their relationship:

1 June 1887. On this day appeared in the Times my letter 'The Universities & national Education'. It did excitedly rejoice me for an hour or two. I rushed into Harry's [his brother] room to show it, & up to Pauline's room to show it—& both rejoiced. It was like a glimpse of 'old joy'.

15 June 1887. (Another moment of depression.) But what an Inferno to be living in! I have under the influence of this spoken very unjustly, intemperately & meanly to my wife. I must try to preserve self-control, the want of it has led to much unhappiness.

19 June 1887. Had a delightful day with Pauline in the country—we went to Ashstead—sate out in the fields—dined at the Swan, returned spirits much better.

A letter Collins left to be opened after his death, written at the time of his voyage to New York (probably with his father's fatal voyage to Melbourne in mind) in December 1893, shows the depth of his feelings for Pauline:

> My Dearest children—Everything in this world being uncertain, and I being on the point of going a long journey, I thought I would like to address a line to you in case it should be the will of God that I should not return. You have had the best mother that children could ever have and I the best wife a man ever had. You will never know all you owe to your dear mother. I entreat you all of you to be good and dutiful children to her as long as you live and she is with you. I exhort you earnestly to love and cherish and to obey her in all things, and to pray always that God will aid you to do your duties well and faithfully all your lives. Your Loving Father.[2]

The marriage, however, clearly got off to an embarrassing start, though it is not known where and when they first met or how their affair developed—if L. C. Collins knew anything about it he kept it to himself. The facts are these: Pauline Strangways, as she still was, gave birth to a son, Laurence Churton, on 25 January 1878; her marriage to Collins took place by licence at the Parish Church of St. Dunstan West in the City of London on 11 April 1878, and their son's birth was finally registered on 28 May 1878. These are the plain facts but they clearly raise a series of intriguing questions: did Collins at first refuse to acknowledge Laurence Churton as his son? Why else was the marriage delayed? Was pressure brought to bear on him to marry Pauline by her father, a solicitor with respectable family connexions? Why was Laurence Churton Collins' birth not registered until 28 May, six weeks after the marriage had taken place? Was the whole affair just another example of Collins' general mismanagement of his life, or did he panic at the thought of taking on new responsibilities at a time when he had no clear prospects and try to evade them? Knowing Collins, one can speculate that the whole thing was a matter of panic and muddle and that the solicitor father came to his daughter's rescue probably giving the couple some financial help. At the time of his father-in-law's death in February 1882, Collins recorded his gratitude in his notebook: 'He was a kind good friend to me. I shall never forget him. Dear Pauline was with me at the funeral. How I shall miss him.'[3]

The marriage as it turned out was a happy one despite all the worries and problems, but in the early days at least it caused Collins some social embarrassments. He was evidently extremely self-conscious about his domestic situation and wrote to Gosse in November 1878, 'It is of course impossible for me to go into society without my wife: it is equally impossible for her & myself living as we do in this unusual ['eccentric' crossed out] way to be of society & therefore we have resolved not to go out except to one or two of her relations, consequently I cannot go out to meet ladies consequently you mustn't ask me.'[4] Collins, quite unfairly of course, must have consciously blamed his wife for all this embarrassment and for hindering his opportunities to meet influential people and this sometimes surfaced in his black moods and bitter outbursts—outbursts of course which were instantly regretted. As time passed, the social embarrassments faded but Collins always seems to have tried to maintain a certain independence from his family ties and responsibilities—spending a good deal of his vacation time in Oxford and elsewhere on his own—as if he felt them to be an encumbrance. At the same time, he was devoted to his wife and family and was always worrying about them. A wife and family, then, acquired perhaps by accident rather than design, brought additional problems and worries to a man already desperately insecure and Collins' wife and family in turn had to bear with someone whose obsession with work and constant depression were partly related to his sense of responsibility for them. The marriage was a happy one but not surprisingly Collins was still fretting about his family responsibilities in his notebook jottings right up to the moment of his death.

NOTES

1　L. C. Collins, op. cit., pp. 36–37.
2　Ibid., pp. 132–33.
3　Ibid., p. 53.
4　Collins to Gosse, MS. letter, dated 4 November 1878. Brotherton Library, University of Leeds.

THE NEW MACAULAY

Collins' style as a reviewer was often likened to Macaulay's by contemporaries and at times he consciously adopted Macaulay's tricks and mannerisms. Some parallel passages from Macaulay and Collins will suggest the influence.

Both reviewers were hypercritical of 'blunders' in facts and dates in the work they reviewed. Here is Macaulay on Croker's edition of Boswell's *Life of Johnson*:

> Nothing in this work has astonished us so much as the ignorance or carelessness of Mr Croker with respect to facts and dates. Many of his blunders are such as we should be surprised to hear any well-educated gentleman commit, even in conversation ... We accuse him of having undertaken a work which, if not performed with strict accuracy, must be very much worse than useless, and of having performed it as if the difference between an accurate and an inaccurate statement was not worth the trouble of looking into the most common book of reference.[1]

Collins borrowed this tone of moral outrage in his review of works by Saintsbury and Gosse; for example, in his review of Saintsbury's *A Short History of English Literature* he wrote:

> It seems impossible to open this book anywhere without alighting on some blunder, or on some inaccuracy ... Many of the Professor's critical remarks can only be explained on the supposition that he assumes that his readers will not take the trouble to verify his references or question his dogmas ... In Professor Saintsbury's eyes such indifference to accuracy may be venial: in our opinion it is nothing less than scandalous. It is assuredly most unfair to those who will naturally expect to find in a book of reference trustworthy information.[2]

Both Macaulay and Collins, of course, were able to use their vast knowledge of literary and historical facts to spot blunders where other reviewers missed them.

Collins also took over something of Macaulay's facetiousness and sarcasm when about to be severe with an author. Here is Macaulay on Dr Edward Nares' monumental Memoirs of Lord Burghley:

> The work of Dr Nares has filled us with astonishment similar to that which Captain Lemuel Gulliver felt when first he landed in Brobdingnag, and saw corn as high as the oaks of the New Forest, thimbles as large as buckets and wrens of the bulk of turkeys. The whole book, and every component part of it, is on a gigantic scale. The title is as long as an ordinary preface: the prefatory matter would furnish out an ordinary book; and the book contains as much reading as an ordinary library. We cannot sum up the merits of the stupendous mass of paper which lies before us better than by saying that it consists of about two thousand closely printed quarto pages, that it occupies fifteen hundred inches cubic measure, and that it weighs sixty pounds avoir-dupois ... Compared with the labour of reading through these volumes, all other labour, the labour of thieves on the treadmill, of children in factories, of negroes in sugar plantations, is an agreeable pastime.[3]

Collins did not have as much space allowed him to adopt the full flavour of Macaulay's leisurely sarcasm, but he often attempted short flights of the same kind; for example, in his remarks on Jusserand's *A Literary History of the English People*, he began

> There is a breeziness and hilarity, a gay irresponsibility and abandon, about M. Jusserand which is perfectly delightful. He is the very Autolycus of History and Criticism. What more sober students, who have some conscience to trouble them, are 'toiling all their lives to find' appears to be his as a sort of natural right. The fertility of his genius is such, that it seems to blossom spontaneously into erudition. Like the lilies he toils not, but unlike the lilies he spins, and very pretty gossamer too.[4]

Both men, in reaction against the diffuseness and vagueness they attacked in other writers, cultivated the vigorous and emphatic statement frequently balancing one statement against another in an extended series of antitheses. Here is Macaulay on Lord Byron:

> In the rank of Lord Byron, in his understanding, in his character, in his very person, there was a strange union of opposite extremes. He was born to all that men covet and admire. But in every one of those eminent advantages which he possessed over others was

mingled something of misery and debasement. He was sprung from a house, ancient indeed and noble, but degraded and impoverished by a series of crimes and follies which had attained a scandalous publicity ... The young peer had great intellectual powers; yet there was an unsound part in his mind. He had naturally a generous and feeling heart: but his temper was wayward and irritable. He had a head which statuaries loved to copy, and a foot the deformity of which beggars in the streets mimicked. Distinguished at once by the strength and by the weakness of his intellect, affectionate yet perverse, a poor lord, and a handsome cripple, he required, if ever man required, the firmest and the most judicious training.[5]

This leads on to a portrait of Byron's mother and another series of antithetical assertions. Collins too liked this mode of description; for example in his portrait of Bolingbroke he wrote:

His virtues and his vices, his reason and his passions, did not as in ordinary men blend themselves in a gradation of tints, but remained isolated in sudden and glaring contrast. His transitions were from extreme to extreme. He was sometimes all vice, he was sometimes all elevation. When his fine intellect was unclouded, his shrewdness and sagacity were a match for De Torcy; his dexterity and adroitness more than a match for Marlborough and Godolphin. When his intellect took the ply from his passions, there was little to distinguish him from the most hot-headed and harebrained of his own tools. In his sublimer moments he out-Catoed Cato, in his less exalted moods he sank below Sandys and Dodington. Etc.[6]

NOTES

1   *Critical and Historical Essays* by Lord Macaulay, 1882, pp. 166–68.
2   *Ephemera Critica*, pp. 101–08.
3   *Critical and Historical Essays* by Lord Macaulay, p. 220.
4   *Ephemera Critica*. p. 193.
5   *Critical and Historical Essays* by Lord Macaulay, p. 148.
6   *Bolingbroke and Voltaire in England*, p. 9.

COLLINS AND CARLYLE

If Macaulay was the most important influence on Collins as a writer and Arnold the most important influence on his thinking about literature, Carlyle was an equally important influence on his philosophical and moral outlook. At Oxford Collins was already reading Carlyle with excited interest and, as we saw in Chapter 2, Carlyle was one of the first writers he approached and interviewed after leaving Balliol. To Carlyle, as much as to Jowett and T. H. Green, Collins owed his strong sense of purpose and mission which kept him going through the exhausting and often demoralizing days of Extension teaching and literary reviewing.

Yet, despite his early admiration for Carlyle, Collins, like others who came under his influence, eventually came to feel that Carlyle's vision of things was too dark and depressing to be acceptable. He readily responded to Carlyle's moral convictions and his 'great force' but his own outlook was basically more hopeful and resilient than Carlyle's. Society might be in a bad way, and Collins of course made a whole career out of denouncing the state of modern life, but he was passionately hopeful, in an un-Carlylean way, about the spread of higher education and the effects this would have on society as a whole: 'during the last few years', he wrote, 'the rapid spread of higher education, the popularization of liberal culture through such agencies as the University Extension Lectures, the National Home Reading Union and similar institutions have called into being an immense and constantly multiplying class of serious readers and students. These already number tens of thousands, they will before long number hundreds of thousands.'[1] This fundamental optimism led him to play down Carlyle's value as a philosopher and guide as time went by, though he never turned on him in the way he turned on Swinburne. This cooler view of Carlyle can be seen in his late essay on 'Emerson's Writings' published in 1912 after his death.

The following passage comparing Carlyle with Emerson is not only interesting for its view of Carlyle but as another example of Macaulay's hypnotic hold on Collins' style:

> We are naturally tempted to institute a comparison between him and his great friend Carlyle. In three great and fundamental points they were alike: both were tremendously in earnest, both were entirely and essentially honest, and both were transcendentalists. But for the rest the comparison lies in contrast. Emerson is an optimist, serene and unfaltering; Carlyle a pessimist, fierce, turbulent, and perverse. To Carlyle the world was peopled mainly with fools and shams; to Emerson the average man had in him the germs and potentialities of the demigods of our race. Carlyle was so diseased and wilful an egotist that though he preached duty and practised what he preached, he neither found any comfort or happiness in it himself, nor did he promise any comfort or happiness in it to any one else; by Emerson's side stood Hope and Faith, transforming Duty and Labour into radiant happiness. Carlyle practically eliminates happiness as a factor in human energy—work, strive, endure, what have you to do with happiness? "what if thou wert born and predestined not to be happy, but to be unhappy?" With Emerson happiness in the true sense of the term is to be sought, to be cherished; it is very sunlight to the soul. It is *always* to the dark side that Carlyle leans; but instinctively as a plant makes for the light does Emerson make for the sun. As a preacher and commentator, Carlyle exhausts the vocabulary of intolerance, despair, and contempt; nothing is so rare in Emerson as any indication of irritability, of intolerance, of sarcasm. Emerson too often misses his mark because he is so vague, so abstract, because he aims too high; but Carlyle's blows have the precision and force of a blacksmith's hammer on his anvil. Carlyle's presentation and expression might be compared to meteoric flashes, lurid, wild, and grand; but we should not go to elementary forces for a simile to apply to presentation and expression in Emerson: rather we should go to a cabinet of gems, finely cut, coldly finished, most exquisitely polished. Into a comparison of the quality and tenor of their writings we need not enter.[2]

NOTES

1 *Ephemera Critica*, pp. 33–34.
2 *The Posthumous Essays of John Charlton Collins*, pp. 164–65.

SELECT BIBLIOGRAPHY

The place of publication is London
unless otherwise indicated

COLLINS' BOOKS

Sir Joshua Reynolds as a Portrait Painter. Macmillan, 1874.
Bolingbroke and Voltaire in England. John Murray, 1886.
Illustrations of Tennyson. Chatto & Windus, 1891.
The Study of English Literature. Macmillan, 1891.
Jonathan Swift. Chatto & Windus, 1893.
Essays and Studies. Macmillan, 1895.
Ephemera Critica. Constable, 1901.
Studies in Shakespeare. Constable, 1904.
Studies in Poetry and Criticism. George Bell, 1905.
Voltaire, Montesquieu and Rousseau in England. Everleigh Nash, 1908.
Greek Influence on English Poetry, ed. Michael Macmillan. Isaac
    Pitman, 1910.
The Posthumous Essays of John Churton Collins, ed. L. C. Collins. J. M.
    Dent, 1912.

WORKS EDITED BY COLLINS

Plays and Poems of Cyril Tourneur. Chatto & Windus, 1878.
Poems of Lord Herbert of Cherbury. Chatto & Windus, 1881.
Milton, *Samson Agonistes.* Clarendon Press, 1883.
Dryden, *Satires.* Clarendon Press, 1893.
Euripides, *Alcestis.* Clarendon Press, 1893.
General editor of Edward Arnold's School *Shakespeare.* 1894.
General editor of Edward Arnold's *British Classics for Schools.* 1895.
Pope, *Essay on Criticism.* Macmillan, 1896.
Treasury of Minor British Poetry. Edward Arnold, 1896.

Early Poems of Lord Tennyson. Methuen, 1899–1901.

Tennyson, *In Memoriam, Princess and Maud.* Methuen, 1902.

Edward Arber's *An English Garner.* Constable, 1903.

Thomas More, *Utopia.* Clarendon Press, 1904.

Plays and Poems of Robert Greene. Clarendon Press, 1905.

Matthew Arnold, *Merope and Sophocles' Electra* (Whitelaw's translation). Clarendon Press, 1906.

Romeo and Juliet, vol. 27 of *Shakespeare's Complete Works.* Renaissance edition, 1906.

Sophocles, *Antigone* (Whitelaw's translation). Clarendon Press, 1906.

Aeschylus, *Agamemnon* (Conington's translation). Clarendon Press, 1907.

Aeschylus, *Prometheus Vinctus* (Whitelaw's translation). Clarendon Press, 1907.

Shelley, *Selected Poems.* T. C. & E. C. Jack, 1907.

Sidney, *Apologie for Poetry.* Clarendon Press, 1907.

UNCOLLECTED ARTICLES BY COLLINS AND MISCELLANEOUS PIECES

'An Educational Crisis and how to avert it', *Pall Mall Gazette*, 28 and 31 May 1886, pp. 1–2 and 11–12.

'English Literature at the Universities', *Quarterly Review*, CLXIII, October 1886, pp. 289–329.

Letters to the *Pall Mall Gazette*: 1 December 1886, signed 'Oxoniensis'; 8 December 1886, signed 'University Extension Lecturer'; 22 January 1887, signed 'A Lover of Truth'.

Letter to *The Times*, 1 June 1887, signed 'A University Extension Lecturer'.

'Philology versus Literature', *Academy*, 17 December 1887, pp. 407–08.

'The Universities in contact with the People', *Nineteenth Century*, XXVI, October 1889, pp.561–83.

'The National Home Reading Union and its Prospects', *Contemporary Review*, LVIII, August 1890, pp. 193–211.

'The New Scheme for the Indian Civil Service Examinations', *Contemporary Review*, LIX, June 1891, pp. 836–51.

'The Ideal University', *Nineteenth Century*, XXXI, February 1892, pp. 243–54.

'The Study of Greek',*University Extension Journal*,15 June 1892, pp. 80–82.

'A Specimen of Oxford Editing', *Saturday Review*, 24 November 1894, pp. 562–3.

'A Professor of English Literature on his own Subject', *Saturday Review*, 30 November 1895, pp. 725–26.

'A Blind Guide in Victorian Literature', *Saturday Review*, 25 April 1896, pp. 423–5.

'The Teaching of English Literature in Schools', *Academy*, 30 January 1897, pp. 150–51.

'Mr Walter Raleigh on Style', *Saturday Review*, 20 November 1897, p. 536.

'A University for the People', *Nineteenth Century*, XLV, March 1899, pp. 465–76.

'The Rhodes Bequest and University Federation', *Nineteenth Century and After*, LVI, December 1904, pp. 970–84.

'Twaddle from a great Scholar', *Saturday Review*,17 February 1906, pp. 205–06.

'The Universities and a School of Journalism', *Nineteenth Century and After*, LXIII, February 1908, pp. 327–40.

OFFICIAL REPORTS AND MANUSCRIPT SOURCES

Report of the Taunton Commission, 21 vols., H.M.S.O., 1868.

London Society for the Extension of University Teaching, *Report of the Council* for 1877 and following years. University of London Library.

London Society, etc., *Reports from Lecturers and Examiners*, 1881 and following years. University of London Library.

University of Oxford Commission, 1877, *Minutes of Evidence*, 1881.

Oxford University: *Minutes of the Committee for University Extension*, 1885–1889. Bodleian Library.

Oxford University Extension: *Lecturers' and Examiners' Reports*, 1886–87. Bodleian Library.

University Extension Congress: *Report of the Proceedings*, 1894.

University of Birmingham, *Calendar*, 1900 and following years.

University of Birmingham, *Report of the Dean of the Faculty of Arts*, 1904 and following years. University of Birmingham Library.

University of London Board to Promote the Extension of University Teaching: *Minutes*, 1905–06. University of London Library.

University of Birmingham, *Minutes of the Boards of Examiners in Arts*, 1904–08. University of Birmingham Library.

The Teaching of English in England, H.M.S.O., 1921.

John Churton Collins, *Notebooks* (1863 and following years). University of Birmingham Library.

Correspondence of Sir Edmund Gosse, Brotherton Library, University of Leeds.

Other MS. letters by Collins are to be found in the Bodleian Library Oxford, the National Library of Scotland and the University of Birmingham Library.

GENERAL SOURCES

Altick, Richard D. *The English Common Reader*. Chicago University Press, 1957.

Anon. 'Professor J. Churton Collins', *Edgbastonia*, March 1906, pp. 47–53.

Anon. Obituary notice of Collins, *The Mermaid*, November 1908, pp. 16–17.

Arnold, Matthew. *Essays in Criticism*, First Series. Macmillan, 1891.

— — *Mixed Essays*. Smith, Elder & Co., 1879.

Letters from Matthew Arnold to John Churton Collins. Privately printed, 1910.

Bennett, Arnold. *Books and Persons*. Chatto & Windus, 1917.

Brewer, D. S. 'English Studies in the University of Birmingham', *English and Germanic Studies*, III, 1949–50, pp. 1–33.

Buckley, J. H. *The Victorian Temper*. Frank Cass, 1952.

Charteris, E. (ed.). *The Life and Letters of Sir Edmund Gosse*, Heinemann, 1931.

Clarke, M. L. *Classical Education in Britain 1500–1900*, Cambridge University Press, 1959.

Collins, L. C. *Life and Memoirs of John Churton Collins*. John Lane, 1912.

De Selincourt, Ernest. Obituary comment on Collins, Birmingham *Daily Post*, 13 October 1909.

Faber, Geoffrey. *Jowett: A Portrait with a Background*. Faber & Faber, 1957.

Gross, John. *The Rise and Fall of the Man of Letters*. Weidenfeld & Nicolson, 1969.

Grosskurth, Phyllis. *John Addington Symonds*. Longmans, 1964.

——'Churton Collins: Scourge of the Late Victorians', *University of Toronto Quarterly*, XXXIV, April 1965, pp. 254–68.

Harris, Frank. *Latest Contemporary Portraits*. The Macaulay Co., New York, 1927.

Lang, Cecil Y. (ed.). *The Swinburne Letters*. 6 vols., Yale University Press, 1959–62.

Leavis, F. R. *Education and the University*. Chatto & Windus, 1943.

Lee, Sidney. 'John Churton Collins', *The Dictionary of National Biography*.

Literary Friend, A. Obituary notice of Collins, *The Times*, 17 September 1908.

Macaulay, Lord. *Critical and Historical Essays*. Longmans, Green & Co., 1882.

MacCarthy, Desmond. *Experience*. Putnam, 1935.

Mallet, C. E. *A History of the University of Oxford*. 3 vols., Methuen, 1927.

Mallock, W. H. *Memoirs of Life and Literature*. Chapman and Hall, 1920.

Matthews, W. R. *Late Victorian Journalistic Criticism*. PhD thesis, Ohio State University, 1961.

Morley, John. *Studies in Literature*. Macmillan, 1890.

Oman, Sir Charles. *Memories of Victorian Oxford*. Methuen, 1941.

Palmer, D. J. *The Rise of English Studies*. Oxford University Press, 1965.

Potter, Stephen. *The Muse in Chains*. Jonathan Cape, 1937.

Powell, Lyman P. 'An English Extension Lecturer', *Harper's Weekly*, 3 February 1894, p. 114.

Raleigh, Lady (ed.). *The Life and Letters of Sir Walter Raleigh*. 2 vols., Methuen, 1926.

Rossetti, W. M. *Some Reminiscences of William Michael Rossetti*. 2 vols., Brown, Langham & Co., 1906.

Saintsbury, George. *George Saintsbury: Essays and Papers*, with a memoir by A. Blyth Webster. Methuen, 1945.

Sparrow, John. *Mark Pattison and the Idea of a University*. Cambridge University Press, 1967.

Theobald, R. M. *The Ethics of Criticism*. Watts & Co., 1904.

Thwaite, Ann. *Edmund Gosse: A Literary Landscape 1849–1928*. Secker, 1984.

Tillyard, E. M. W. *The Muse Unchained*. Bowes & Bowes, 1958.

Vincent, Eric W. and Hinton, Percival. *The University of Birmingham*. Cornish Brothers, Birmingham, 1947.

Wellek, René. *A History of Modern Criticism 1750–1950*. Vol. 4., 'The Later Nineteenth Century'. Jonathan Cape, 1966.

INDEX

Academy, 47, 72, 114
Allen, Grant, 74
Archer, William, 64
Arnold, Matthew, 7, 14, 16, 74, 80, 93, 128, 129, 150–54, 155, 156
Asquith, Herbert, 7, 8, 147
Athenaeum, 60, 64, 66

Balliol College, 7–8
Bennett, Arnold, 161–62
Birmingham University, 120–25, 132, 137–43, 145–47
Blackwood's Magazine, 22–23
Bodington, Nathan, 147
Bradley, A.C., 47, 118, 135
Brewer, D.S., 135
Bright, John, 73
British Weekly, 139
Browning, Robert, 7, 16, 18, 28–29

Cambridge University, 46, 72
Carlyle, Thomas, 12, 13, 20–21, 25, 80, 129, 152, 174–75
Church, Dean, 113
Churton, John, 2
Churton, Maria, 1
Clough, A.H., 7
Collins, Henry Ramsay, 1–2
Collins, John Churton:
  early life and education, 1–16
  literary contacts, 18–29
  marriage, 36, 168–70
  Extension career, 36–46, 82, 83, 85, 105, 118, 137–38
  applications for university posts, 46–50, 116, 120

quarrels with Symonds, Swinburne and Gosse, 52–67
Oxford campaign, 70–85, 113–114
reviewing for the *Saturday*, 106–12
Professor at Birmingham, 120–48
School of Journalism, 139–43
on Classics, 43, 44, 61, 72, 81, 84, 122–24, 154–56
on Anglo-Saxon, 44, 48–50, 61, 122
Books and works edited: *Sir Joshua Reynolds as a Portrait Painter*, 22 *Plays and Poems of Cyril Tourneur*, 24, 157 *Poems of Lord Herbert of Cherbury*, 27, 157 *Essays and Studies*, 27, 59, 88, 98–103, 105 *Bolingbroke and Voltaire in England*, 30 *Voltaire, Montesquieu and Rousseau in England*, 31, 125 *Plays and Poems of Robert Greene*, 59, 157 *The Study of English Literature*, 80, 82, 88, 89, 124, 150, 154, 160, 165 *Illustrations of Tennyson*, 88–92, 94, 155, 161 *Jonathan Swift*, 93–98 *Ephemera Critica*, 112–16, 145, 159, 160, 165 *Studies in Shakespeare*, 125–29, 158 *Studies in Poetry and Criticism*, 125, 129–32 *Greek Influence on English Poetry*, 125 151 *Posthumous Essays*, 125, 175 Milton's *Samson Agonistes*, 157 Pope's *Essay on Criticism*, 157

Sidney's *Apologie for Poetrie*, 157

death, 143–44

reputation, 160–62

Collins, Pauline, née Strangways, 36, 148, 168–70

Collins, L.C., 36, 144, 168–69

Contemporary Review, 77

Cornhill, 23, 27, 88, 102

Courthope, W.J., 27, 40, 74, 93, 116, 117

Craik, Henry, 93, 95, 98, 117

Curzon, Lord, 147

Daily News, 18

Daily Post, 139

Daniel, Dr. R., 143

Day, J.D., 3

De Selincourt, Ernest, 114, 146–47

Dixon, W. Macneile, 118, 120, 122

Dobson, Austin, 25

Dowden, Edward, 47, 116, 117, 120, 165

Doyle, Arthur Conan, 133, 134, 147

Dryden, John, 99–100

Earle, John, 77, 116

Echo, 92

Edwards, John Passmore, 113

Eliot, T.S., 24

Evans, Charles, 4

Extension Movement, 37–44, 75–76, 83, 137–38

Fiedler, H.G., 120

Forbes, Mansfield, 154, 164

Forster, John, 93

Freeman, E.A., 77–78

Froude, J.A., 33

Furnivall, F.J., 117

Garnett, Richard, 110

Gilzean-Reid, Sir Hugh, 142

Gissing, George, 40, 163, 167·

Gladstone, W.E., 73

Globe, 18, 133

Gordon, Peter, 17

Goschen, G.J., 47, 75, 165

Gosse, Edmund, 1, 23, 25–27, 46, 47, 52, 60–67, 69, 74, 107, 108, 137, 147, 153, 159, 160, 164, 165, 170

Green, T.H., 7, 12–13, 136, 174

Greg, W.W., 125

Grosart, A.B., 24

Gross, John, 33, 167

Grosskurth, Phyllis, 68, 167

Hales, J.W., 38, 116

Harper's Weekly, 85

Harris, Frank, 33, 106, 161

Harrison, Frederic, 17, 113

Henley, W.E., 109

Hopkins, Gerard Manley, 7

Huxley, T.H., 73

Indian Civil Service Examinations, 19

Jebb, R.C., 116

Jeffrey, Francis, 55

Jowett, Benjamin, 11–12, 16, 19, 74, 113, 165, 174

Jusserand, J.J., 102–3, 172

Ker, W.P., 49, 118

King Edward's School Birmingham, 4–7

Kingsley, Charles, 26

Lang, Andrew, 7, 8, 18, 116, 117, 165

Leavis, F.R., 104, 164–65, 167

Lee, Sidney, 72, 93, 101, 159, 166

Le Gallienne, Richard, 60, 92, 103, 113, 160

Lodge, Oliver, 120, 132

London Society for the Extension of University Teaching, 38–44, 75–76, 137

Lounsbury, T.R., 117

Lowell, J.R., 126
Luce, Mrs. Edmund, 13
Macaulay, T.B., 19, 32–33, 55, 66, 102, 158, 171–73, 175
MacCarthy, Desmond, 161
Mallock, W.H., 7, 11, 12, 17
Marston, Philip, 25
Massey, Gerald, 130
Massingham, H.W., 136
Menander, 102
Mermaid, 146
Modern Language Review, 125
Monro, D.B., 76
Morley, Henry, 38, 40, 49, 108, 116
Morley, John, 31, 85, 147, 158
Morris, William, 74
Moulton, R.G., 38, 43, 45, 156, 162
Müller, Max, 73

Napier, A.S., 47, 48, 146
Nation, 139
National Review, 133
Nicoll, Sir William Robertson, 139
Nineteenth Century, 78, 83

O'Shaughnessy, Arthur, 25

Oxford University:
  examination schools, 9, 81
  reforms, 10–11
  Merton Chair of English, 47–49, 70
  views on English studies, 70–72, 74–78
  School of Modern Languages, 72, 75–76
  Extension Committee, 76, 138
  English School, 83, 113–14
  Chair of English Literature, 84, 116
Oxford Magazine, 48, 67, 71, 75, 113, 114

Palgrave, F.T., 7
Pall Mall Gazette, 32, 61, 64, 72, 74, 75, 76, 77, 115, 134, 153

Palmer, D.J., 51, 70, 86, 87, 119
Pater, Walter, 56, 74
Pattison, Mark, 27–28, 63, 93, 113, 165
Pattison, Robert, 103
Phillips, Stephen, 20, 132, 136, 163
Philology, 48, 61, 71, 72, 73, 83, 156
Potter, Stephen, 70
Potts, Dr. A., 2, 4

Quarterly Review, 26, 27, 30, 55, 60, 61, 64, 66, 74–75

Raleigh, W.A., 60, 117–18, 132, 160, 162
Rhys, John, 116, 117
Roberts, R.D., 138
Rossetti, W.M., 107

Saintsbury, George, 1, 27, 102, 108–12, 158, 162, 171
Saturday Review, 27, 33, 60, 82, 102, 106–12, 118, 138, 145, 161
Scoones, W.B., 19, 45, 47
Shairp, J.C., 7
Shaw, G.B., 106
Shorter, Clement, 139
Skeat, Walter, 47, 71
Smith, Dr. William, 27, 47
Sonnenschein, E.A., 121, 122–24, 155
Spectator, 82, 92, 150
Spender, J.A., 143
Stead, W.T., 72, 75, 86, 134
Stephen, Leslie, 27, 47, 85, 93, 98, 113, 117, 158, 165
Stuart, James, 37
Sweet, Henry, 47, 51, 72, 121
Swinburne, A.C., 7, 21, 23–25, 29, 33, 56–60, 61, 62, 65–67, 73, 98, 103, 137, 147, 148, 160, 163, 164, 165
Symonds, John Addington, 1, 7, 23, 52, 55–60, 62, 64, 66, 73, 98, 130, 160, 165

Symons, Arthur, 1, 115, 160, 163

Tennyson, Alfred Lord, 52, 64, 73, 88–92, 101, 155, 161
Theobald, Lewis, 100–1
Theobald, R.M., 135
The Teaching of English in England, 155
Thorley, G.E., 76
Tillyard, E.M.W., 154
Times, 74, 120, 146

University Extension Journal, 82

Warren, T.H., 118
Watson, William, 130–31, 132, 145, 163
Watts-Dunton, Theodore, 25, 66, 68, 148, 160
Welch, Edwin, 50
Wellek, René, 50
Wells, H.G., 106
White, John, 17
Wise, T.J., 160

Yeats, W.B., 163, 167